It's Our Research

Getting Stakeholder Buy-in for User Experience Research Projects

It's Our Research

Getting Stakeholder Buy-in for User Experience Research Projects

TOMER SHARON

Foreword by Rolf Molich

AMSTERDAM • BOSTON • HEIDELBERG • LONDON
NEW YORK • OXFORD • PARIS • SAN DIEGO
SAN FRANCISCO • SINGAPORE • SYDNEY • TOKYO

Morgan Kaufmann is an imprint of Elsevier

Acquiring Editor: Steve Elliot
Development Editor: David Bevans
Project Manager: Danielle S. Miller
Designer: Kristen Davis

Morgan Kaufmann is an imprint of Elsevier
225 Wyman Street, Waltham, MA 02451, USA

Library of Congress Cataloging-in-Publication Data
Sharon, Tomer.
 It's our research : getting stakeholder buy-in for user experience research projects / Tomer Sharon. – 1st ed.
   p. cm.
  ISBN 978-0-12-385130-7
 1. Human-computer interaction. 2. User interfaces (Computer systems) I. Title. II. Title: Getting stakeholder buy-in for user experience research projects.
 QA76.9.H85S494 2012
 005.4'37–dc23   2011044873

British Library Cataloguing-in-Publication Data
A catalogue record for this book is available from the British Library

ISBN: 978-0-12-385130-7

Printed in China
12 13 14 15   10 9 8 7 6 5 4 3 2 1

For information on all MK publications visit our website at www.mkp.com

To my life, Iris.

To my boys, Segev and Sella. I love you to the moon, sky, stars, sun, clouds, and back.

PRAISE FOR *IT'S OUR RESEARCH*

"There is probably no question that I am asked more often than "How can I have more influence?" User research that isn't able to bring insight and drive improvement might as well not have happened. This book is the most complete guide to getting stakeholder buy-in that I have seen. It is a 'must read' for researchers and their managers."—**Arnie Lund, Microsoft**; **Author,** *User Experience Management*

"Tomer Sharon's book is the cure for usability professionals whose work isn't having the impact it deserves. Here you'll find ways to work different, to make your research connect with stakeholders instead of trash cans. File under: work smarter, not harder."—**Gerard Torenvliet, Senior Human Factors Scientist, Medtronic**

"*It's Our Research* should be required reading for anyone involved in a UX research study. Sharon will not only help you avoid the many pitfalls that most UX research projects come across, but more importantly give you all the tips and tricks for getting the most out your UX research."—**William Albert, Bentley University; Author,** *Measuring the User Experience* **and** *Beyond the Usability Lab*

"As an experienced Human Factors Engineer, I thought I knew how to do user research and engage stakeholders. But in these pages I discovered new ways to ensure my user research will be useful to my clients. The book is well organized and includes rich interviews and case study content. I especially appreciated the takeaways at the end of each chapter."—**Stan Caplan, President, Usability Associates, LLC**

"If no one reads your report or implements your recommendations does it really matter how statistically valid your findings were? Do yourself and your users a favor ... read Tomer's Book."—**Jeff Sauro, Principal Measuring Usability LLC; Author,** *Quantifying the User Experience*

CONTENTS

3 IF YOU PICK A METHODOLOGY FIRST, SOMETHING MUST BE WRONG 67

Strategies for planning studies with stakeholders and techniques for developing the right research questions

4 WHAT'S GONNA WORK? TEAMWORK! 101
Hands-on techniques for collaborating and involving stakeholders in research planning, execution, analysis, and reporting

5

THE SINGLE BIGGEST PROBLEM IN COMMUNICATION IS THE ILLUSION THAT IT HAS TAKEN PLACE 149
Strategies and tools to effectively communicate research results by using reports, presentations, and more cool stuff

6 YOU CAN'T MANAGE WHAT YOU DON'T MEASURE 209

Signs that indicate research is being used well and how you can systematically track success (or failure)

FOREWORD

By Rolf Molich

Have you ever heard the sayings "The cobbler's children have no shoes" or "The plumber has leaky faucets"? Have you smiled at them, assuring yourself that most usability professionals are far above such trivial, conventional problems?

I have bad and good news for you.

The bad news is that my research shows that a considerable number of products produced by usability professionals are hard to use or don't meet their users' needs. I've encountered unusable usability test reports, unusable personas, unusable interview reports, and unusable websites of companies who sell usability services. And even worse than that: some of us are not very good at selling and communicating our knowledge and our deliverables to people who are not usability professionals.

The good news is that some people are starting to discuss these problems openly. The book that you have in your hands right now, *It's Our Research*, is one of the important milestones on the road to making usability products truly usable and increasing their impact.

As good usability professionals, we must respect and follow the rules that we preach to others, including knowing your users, designing with your users, and iterating.

By "users," I don't mean end users. End users are very important, of course. But even more important for your success are the direct users of your deliverables: the development team, the marketing team, your management team, and so on.

Usability is maturing. Twenty years ago, Joe Dumas, Ginny Redish, and Jeffrey Rubin advanced the usability testing field when they almost simultaneously published *A Practical Guide to Usability Testing* (Dumas and Redish, originally published in 1993) and *The Handbook of Usability Testing* (Rubin, 1994).

Today, I have a whole bookshelf of literature about usability testing and user research. Specialized usability testing books like *Moderating Usability Tests* by Dumas and Loring (2008) and *Remote Research* by Bolt and Tulathimutte (2010) are starting to appear, indicating the need for our services.

But it's not just the usability profession that is maturing. The consumers of usability products are maturing, too. Some of our users are getting so mature that they no longer accept just anything in the name of usability. They demand quality. In response to bad experiences with professional usability services, they define rigorous and reasonable standards for usability testing, expert reviews, interviews, personas, and more. They set up extensive quality assurance programs to ensure that they get what they pay for. You can no longer do whatever you want in the name of usability.

It's a widespread myth that people who criticize usability are evil or irrational enemies of a good cause. Sure, I've met people who fanatically believed things like, "Cowboy programmers don't need no stinkin' usability," or "If it was hard to code, it must be hard to use," or "You can't teach a pig to sing — and trying to just annoys the pig" (about users' inability to learn to use an unusable website). But my experience is that a majority of the people who criticize my work are not just right – they are also acting in the best interest of all of us. Usability professionals make mistakes – and they are not always good at iterating: listening openly to feedback from others, learning from their mistakes, and applying their own methods to themselves in order to improve their work practices.

This book, *It's Our Research*, fills a gap on my bookshelf. Other books have assumed that once you've carried out a usability activity, the results will sell themselves. Tomer Sharon has done a great job of compiling useful wisdom on how to make usability useful and usable. He has interviewed a large number of knowledgeable people and combined his findings with his own great insight.

The contents of this book can be summarized in seven words: do as you preach and be humble. If that's not sufficiently usable for you, and you want more details, read on!

ACKNOWLEDGMENTS

Authoring a book is an amazing experience. It would not have been possible without many good people who lent a hand. Their names belong on the cover as much as mine.

It all started in downtown Portland, Oregon, thanks to Daniel Szuc and Josephine Wong. I joined you for lunch – and see what happened. Dan, our conversations helped me overcome many blocks. Thank you.

It continued with the persistence of Morgan Kaufmann's acquisition editor, Mary James, who showed me the way.

My reviewers were amazing. They gave me confidence and excellent advice and spanked my behind when I needed it. Thank you to Gerard Torenvliet, Bill Albert, Jeff Sauro, and Stan Caplan. This book is excellent because of you and bad because of me.

Morgan Kaufmann's Rachel Roumeliotis, Steve Elliot, and especially Dave Bevans are the professionals that make things happen. I highly appreciate what you do and thank you for it.

Thank you to Gary Bunker for allowing me to include The Usable Planet in the book.

I wanted this book to mix the knowledge and experience of many people. I thank all those who took the time to write a case study. The experience you share is invaluable: Scott Smith, Gerry Gaffney, Moshe Ingel, Eva Kaniasty, Hiroshi Ushioda, Susumu Kuriyama, Reva Hamon, Gregg Almquist, Michael Summers, Richard Buttiglieri, Lior Yair, Vitaly Mijiritsky, Bill Albert, Silvia Zimmermann, Carol Smith, Kris Engdahl, Jen McGinn, Jakob Biesterfeldt, Meena Kothandaraman, Jeff Sauro, Shmuel Bollen, Yoram Pomer, Steve Portigal, Julie Norvaisas, Kirsten Robinson, Sauli Laitinen, Amir Dotan, Stephen Denning, Takashi Sasaki, Beverly Freeman, Chris Hass, Filip Healy, Roland Stahel, Bob Thomas, Michael Hawley, Michele Visciola, Aga Bojko, and Rolf Molich.

Thank you to Gustavo Moura, Manu Cornet, and Nate Bolt for allowing me to use your pictures and comics and to Josephine Wong, Joseph Marburger, Joshua Ledwell, Tawheed Kader, Livia Labate, Arnie Lund, and Scott Berkun for your tweets.

The most exciting part of authoring this book was the video interviews and contributions. I learned so much from all of you and know that now anyone can enjoy your wisdom. Thank you to Jay Trimble, Paul Adams, Aza Raskin, Donna Tedesco, Jeff Sauro, Jared Spool, Leah Buley, Cennydd Bowles, Dana Chisnell, Donna Spencer, Takashi Sasaki, Caroline Jarrett, Ido Mor, Kim Goodwin, Rolf Molich, Giles Colborne, Meena Kothandaraman, Whitney Hess, Eric Ries, Janice Fraser, Johanna Kollmann, William Gribbons, Ben Shneiderman, Chris St. Hilaire, Gerry McGovern, Bertice Berry, Filip Healy, Felipe Caro, Ruben van Loosbroek, Maartje van Hardeveld, and Guy Winch.

Many people at Google deserve my acknowledgement. I especially thank my reviewers, Dan Russel, Noam Wolf, and John Boyd, who worked hard on top of having a life.

A special thanks to Kristen Davis who designed a beautiful book and to Aviel Lazar for the QR codes idea.

Last, Iris. You are the love of my life. This book would have remained a dream without your support. For that I thank you from the bottom of my heart. I look forward to many more years of making our dreams a reality. I hope not too many of them involve alarm clocks going off at 4:00 a.m.

#humbled

ABOUT THE AUTHOR

Tomer is a user experience researcher, speaker, writer, and leader. He is working at Google in New York, supporting Google Search with UX research. Previously, he led the user experience research effort for Google's online advertising management platform, DFP (Doubleclick for Publishers). Prior to Google, he worked as a user researcher at Check Point Software Technologies in Israel. As founder and first president of UPA Israel, he led the chapter to many achievements such as raising awareness of the need for easy-to-use, efficient, and fun technology products and growing and nurturing a professional community of 1,000 practitioners.

Tomer is an experienced speaker at local and international conferences, a published author of articles and papers, and a past editorial board member for UPA's *UX Magazine*.

His taste in music includes Coldplay, Green Day, the Fray, the Killers, the Postal Service, Snow Patrol, and U2. He is a Boston Red Sox and Hapoel Tel Aviv fan, and an ex-paraglider.

Tomer holds a BA in Social Sciences from the Open University and a master's degree in Human Factors in Information Design from Bentley University in Waltham, Massachusetts.

LIST OF FIGURES AND TABLES

Figures

Tables

CASE STUDIES

Chapter	Author	Title	Country	Page
5	Beverly Freeman	Taking advantage of the theory of psychology and human factors	United States	202
6	Michele Visciola	Better buying experience for blackberry phones	Italy	210
6	Tomer Sharon	What happened when i invited executives to use the product?	United States	213
6	Agnieszka (Aga) Bojko	Why?	United States	221
Epilogue	Rolf Molich	Quality and usability	Denmark	232

VIDEOS

QR Code Number	Interviewee	Country
111	Jay Trimble	United States
112	Paul Adams	United States
113	Aza Raskin	United States
114	Donna Tedesco	United States
115	Jeff Sauro	United States
116	Jared Spool	United States
117	Leah Buley	United States
118	Cennydd Bowles	United Kingdom
119	Dana Chisnell	United States
120	Donna Spencer	Australia
121	Takashi Sasaki	Japan
122	Caroline Jarrett	United Kingdom
123	Ido Mor	United States
124	Kim Goodwin	United States
125	Rolf Molich	Denmark
126	Giles Colborne	United Kingdom
127	Meena Kothandaraman	United States
128	Whitney Hess	United States
129	Eric Ries	United States
130	Janice Fraser	United States
131	Johanna Kollmann	United Kingdom
132	William Gribbons	United States
133	Ben Shneiderman	United States
134	Chris St. Hilaire	United States
135	Gerry McGovern	Ireland
136	Bertice Berry	United States
137	Amberlight Partners	United Kingdom
138	Rabobank Group	Netherlands
139	Guy Winch	United States

ONLINE PRESENCE

	Companion site itsourresear.ch	
amazon.com®	Amazon http://goo.gl/ohEhY	
BARNES & NOBLE BOOKSELLERS	Barnes & Noble http://goo.gl/f18ao	
Google+	Google+ http://goo.gl/phOjF	
	Twitter book http://twitter.com/itsourresearch	
	Twitter author http://twitter.com/tsharon	
	Facebook http://facebook.com/itsourresearch	
You**Tube** Broadcast Yourself™	YouTube http://goo.gl/wUUQ2	

vimeo	Vimeo http://goo.gl/xo2EK	
LANYRD	Lanyrd http://goo.gl/GkRdB	
flickr	Flickr http://goo.gl/fROAw	

PROLOGUE

THE USABLE PLANET

Gary Bunker

Why Is This Story a Part of the Book?

I don't know Gary. We have never met. I first read this story when I was a young, inexperienced practitioner. It made me laugh and think a lot. I believe this story, ignoring for a minute how fun it is to read, delivers an important message. It demonstrates extremely well what's going to happen if user experience practitioners don't work hand in hand with stakeholders in UX research. We researchers and usability people want to make the world a better place. This story is an excellent reminder of what might happen if we work not with stakeholders but against them.

Recording 1

Day 1.

I've been asked to keep this journal, and to record everything that happens to me each day. I've had some problems figuring this little device out, but I think it's working now. Let me . . . yes, I can see the text coming up on the little screen. Okay.

Um, let me see, well, I woke up this morning in a glass tube. The last thing I remember I was in St Mary's Hospital, Portsmouth, England. Waiting to die from the illness that I'd been fighting. This morning I wake up in this bizarre cylinder . . .

I couldn't get out at first. There was a button on the inside, just above my head, but my arms were locked at my sides so I couldn't reach it. It was hours until someone walked into the room and I got their attention and they let me out.

This is going to sound crazy – at least, it sounds crazy to me – but they told me that the year was 2367! Apparently I was cryogenically frozen back in 1999, and I've been in that tube ever since! They say they've cured the cancer and that I'm going to be fine – I can hardly believe this, but it's true – I'm just going to lie down now, I feel exhausted.

Recording 2

Still day 1, I think. I'm in a room now; it looks like a hospital room, though I don't recognize any of the machines. There's a machine that looks like it serves coffee over there, boy I could do with a good coffee – hold on a sec . . .

Beep Ow!!! Oh, you ***Beep*** machine!

Damn! Sorry, I touched the front of the machine and it spat boiling hot coffee all over me! Jeez, it's scalded my chest; it must be broken or – hold on, here comes a nurse. ***Paused***

Resumed That's better. She put some cream on it and the pain is going away now. She laughed when I told her what had happened. Apparently you have to set the direction of your cup and the type of coffee you want before you touch the panel on the front. There's buttons on the top for that, but I didn't see them. I told her that was a dumb design and pretty dangerous, but she said it was just because I haven't been around since the big change. When I asked what she meant, she said that back in 2022 there was a revolt. The programmers and designers of the world executed all the HCI (human–computer interaction) and Usability experts, and since then there had been nothing standing in the way of designers building the best products. She said I just had to get used to things being a little different.

Oh well, I'll be more careful next time – I guess I've got a lot to learn here! I still can't get over the fact that it's 2367 . . .

Recording 3

Sorry I've not recorded for a whole day, they've been testing me and asking me questions all day. It's now day 3 but the good news is that they've said I can walk around the hospital now. I'm not allowed to go outside just yet, not until I've acclimatized and they are sure there are no further problems, but just getting out of this room is going to be great! ***Paused***

Resumed Well, my first outing was less than successful. The floor I'm on is pretty much empty, but there's a lift at the end of the hall. It looked pretty much like lifts from 1999, but there's no button to call it. I stood around waiting for it until it just kind of arrived, so I got in – but there were no buttons inside.

I thought it might be voice activated, you know, like on *Star Trek*, but no matter what I said it just sat there. In the end the doors opened again, and red lights started to flash. I was pretty embarrassed so I just came back here to my room. I feel like an idiot in this place . . .

Recording 4

Okay, day 4. That lift isn't going to beat me. I asked the nurse, and she said that a personal navigator activated it. She gave me one; it's this tiny little pad that inter-acts with the building you're in. It shows you where you are, lists what's in the building and you can use it to tell the lifts where you are going. She said it's great, because you don't need to worry about floors any more; you just need to know your destination. I'm going to try it today. ***Paused***

Resumed Well, I'm ready. I've set the personal navigator to take me to the rooftop café, it's a lovely day out there – I'm off!

Uh, okay, I'm at the lift and waiting. I guess it just – oh! Here it is, okay, stepping into the lift now . . . The doors are closing . . . And we're off! This is so cool!

Going up, going up . . .

Ah. The lift has just stopped and the doors aren't opening. I must have done some-thing wrong. Let me just . . . No, I've set the destination again. I think I've got the right button, but nothing's happening. No emergency telephone. Oh ***Beep*** . . .

Okay, don't panic, don't panic. I'll just keep pressing buttons. There's no labels or anything, just funny little squiggles on them. I wish they'd tell me what all these do! I'll just keep messing around until someth—Oh! Jeez, it's going up again but it's moving pretty fast, oh way too fast! Hoooolllyyyy craaaaaaaa- ***Beep*** Ouch, oh my ***Beep*** "Violent motion will damage this device, please refrain from throwing it to the ground."

Recording 5

I am not happy.

That ***Beep*** ***Beep*** personal organizer somehow crashed the lift into the roof of the hospital! They had to call the police!!!

How the hell do they expect people to use those things? The nurses had to do some fast-talking to stop the police from dragging me away for criminal damage, then they had to fix me up again – I bounced off the roof of the lift when it hit! My head still hurts . . . I'm not going to let it beat me, though; I'm going to get that lift working if it kills me.

Recording 6

Day 7. They've told me to stay put in bed while they teach me the "basics" of life in this new world. They look at me like I'm backward or something. I hate it. But I'll prove them wrong today. They didn't take away my personal navigator, and I've been playing with it. It's hellishly hard to understand but I think I have the gist of it. I'm going to use it today and get that damn lift to take me down to the gardens. I want to be out in the open air again.

Wish me luck.

Recording 7

Okay! I'm in the lift and it's going down. There's no counter so it's hard to say, but I think we must be getting near the ground now. It's slowing down. Slowing down . . . the doors are opening!

Right! Oh . . . ***Beep***

You're not going to believe this. I didn't quite get it right; I ended up in what looks like a basement level rather than at ground. Close, but no cigar.

The lift had already closed behind me before I realized. I've been waiting for it to come back, but it must be busy. ***Paused***

Resumed Haven't got a watch but it feels like half an hour since I got here, and still no lift. What's keeping the damn thing? ***Paused***

Resumed Jeez! It's been hours and the damn lift won't come back! I've had a good look around the place but there's no other way out, and nothing I can figure out that will help me, no phones. I banged on some pipes for a while, but nobody came. I'll just have to wait for the lift. I have to remain calm.

Recording 8

Beep ***Beep*** ***Beep*** you ***Beep*** lift!!!!

Recording 9

Two days!!! Two *days* I was down there!!! I hate that lift so much!!! I'm *never* going in a lift again till the day I die!

Recording 10

Okay, I'm a little calmer now. It's day – 15, I think. They've taught me a lot of the basics, as they call it, and they say I can now go out into the world. Apparently I don't need to work and all food and services are free, so I just need to find a place to live. They're organizing an apartment for me today and I should be able to go there tomorrow. I've asked them to make sure the building has stairs.

Free at last!!!

Recording 11

Today is the day! I'm now in my own apartment! It has a fantastic view out over this city – they say it's London, though it doesn't look like it to me. Wow, this city has changed . . .

They showed me around, but it's pretty basic – a small kitchen area, a bedroom, and a large living area with a picture window looking out over the city. I'm a long way up; I think it was the 69th floor, but it's hard to tell; because of these damn personal navigator things, they don't think floor numbers are important any more and took them all down.

So, I have a home, and I don't need money – apparently they've done away with money and taxes and everything else; everything is free. I just need to figure out what to do next . . .

Recording 12

There's a TV here! I didn't think they'd still have TV, but there's a huge one hidden in the wall. I found it when I tried to turn the lights off. Now how do you turn it on . . . ? Ah.

Hey, lovely picture! Oops. Volume is going up, I must be standing on the remote or something . . . it keeps getting louder . . . Damn! How do I . . . ?

Won't turn off! It's GETTING TOO LOUD! I CAN'T ***Unintelligible response, please rephrase your statement*** . . . "Mary, I love you, can't you see that?" . . . "But Hank, I love Starla and I'll always be hers, you must know you can't tear us apart! I'm going to live with her on Mars and raise . . . " [unintelligible] / [unintelligible] . . . ***Paused***

Resumed If I ever meet the guy who designed that TV, I'm going to ram a personal navigator so far up his ***Beep*** he'll be going up and down in lifts for months! That damn TV wouldn't turn off and wouldn't turn down, in the end the guy from next door burst in and turned it off for me. Apparently you turn it on by touch, and then the volume goes up until you say a command – "Level," I think he said. I didn't know the command, so it just kept getting louder and louder. You then operate the thing completely by voice commands. Stupid! Absolutely stupid! What the *hell* were they thinking when they designed the thing?

No more TV for me. I'm going to bed.

Recording 13

I hate this place already. I found the shower, but can I get the hot water to flow? No.

Can I find towels? No. I had to have a cold shower and then dry myself with the bedclothes. I'm not asking for help though, I've made myself look stupid enough already. I'm going to figure this century out; it can't be much harder than this, it really can't. If I can just understand how their designers think . . . ***Paused***

Resumed Next challenge. Breakfast. I'm calm, and I'm thinking rationally. There *has* to be a design process here, something that makes it obvious if I just think like them.

The food dispenser is in a corner in the kitchen. A little glass door similar to the one at the hospital, but they never showed me how to work that. I've tried voice commands but so far no luck. I've felt all over it, but no buttons or controls I can see.

Stay calm, stay calm . . . ***Paused***

Resumed Two hours. Two hours I've been working at that thing, trying to get food out of it. Not a word, not a beep.

Then it gets up, rolls across the room, and starts hoovering the floor.

IT'S A GODDAMN VACUUM CLEANER!!!

Recording 14

I haven't eaten all day and I'm starving; I'm going out to eat. There must be somewhere to eat in this city. Let me see . . . no key or lock on the door; I guess it just recognizes me like the doors at the hospital. Okay, it's a warm day, don't need a coat. I'm off!

Ah. ***Paused***

Resumed Okay, I asked for a building with stairs and this one has stairs.

Only they put me on the 69th floor, didn't they . . . Oh ***Beep***.

All right, I'm not taking the lift; I'll walk it. I'm pretty fit, and I've got all day. It's not a problem . . . really . . . ***Paused***

Resumed . . . ooooh . . . I . . . I can't walk anymore . . . Got to . . . stop . . .

Ah! Hey . . . ! Hello there . . . Can you . . . can you tell me what . . . what floor . . . this is? Oh ***Beep*** . . . I'm only on 31, I've still . . . got 31 floors to go . . . . And then I've got to climb back up 69 floors to get home! ***Paused***

Resumed Right, this is silly. I've got my breath back, though I don't think my legs will ever work right again. I have to learn how to use that lift, there's nothing else to do.

Okay, I'm at the lift. Waiting . . . it's opening, right, now my personal – oh no, I didn't bring it! Damn damn damn damn!!!!

NO! The lift's going up! NO!!!!! ***Beep*** ***Beep*** ***Beep*** ***Beep*** ***Beep*** ***Beep*** ***Beep*** ***Beep*** . . .

[unintelligible] . . . no, it's okay, I'm getting out . . . what floor is this? 82 . . . thank you . . . ***Paused***

Resumed I'm back where I started. I'm back at the apartment. But the ***Beep*** ***Beep*** door won't open for me!!! Oh man, I hate this place!!!

Recording 15

Next morning. Don't ask me what day it is, I've lost count. I haven't eaten in two days and I've just had a cold shower. Didn't bother to dry off this time. What's the point?

I had to get the neighbor to call the police for me. They did something to the lock and spent a long time laughing at me. Didn't I know that I had to set a password before I left? Didn't they have doorway passwords back in the "Stone Age"? Would I like them to arrange a babysitter for me?

The one slightly positive thing I got out of it was that I do have a food dispenser after all – it's the weird picture thing over the thing that looks like a washing machine but probably isn't. One of the cops made a doughnut and coffee while the other was fixing the door. Some things never change.

So this morning I'm going to get my breakfast at least . . . Now, how did he do it? ***Paused***

Resumed Okay, I'm getting somewhere. When I touched it, the front went black and lit up a numeric pad. I guess I must enter the code for the food I want. Now all I need is a list of codes. There must be one around here somewhere . . . breakfast here I come! ***Paused***

Resumed Okay, no codes. No ***Beep*** codes. But that's okay, I can do this. I'll just keep typing numbers in till some food pops out. Right about now I don't care what comes out; I'll eat anything. ***Paused***

Resumed I got it!!! It's lighting up inside, it's making something!!! It looks like, like . . .

Beep

Recording 16

Cat food.

Of all the codes I could have hit, I hit cat food. I've got three bowls of it so far, different flavors but all cat food. Nothing else.

And you know, I'm starting to actually look at that food . . . ***Paused***

Resumed Come on, come on . . . please!!! Give me something, anything but cat food!!!!

Beep ***Beep*** ***Beep*** ***Beep*** ***Beep*** I HATE THIS WORLD!!!

Oh, I've got to stop for a minute, my finger is killing me from poking random numbers into this thing. If I just have a cup of coffee, maybe I'll be a bit fresher, maybe I'll be able to ***Beep*** oh OW!!!!! ***Beep*** ***Beep*** you damn ***Beep*** machine I'm going to ***Beep*** your ***Beep*** right out the window! I forgot the buttons on the top again! That's it . . . you're going out the window you little piece of junk . . . where's the window catch . . . . Oh come on! Just open you – / ***Beep*** [Unintelligible] . . . "Violent motion will damage this device, please refrain from throwing it to the ground"

Addendum: London Local News

". . . And on a lighter note, a man was found dead in South London today, after apparently throwing himself from the 69th story attached to his coffee machine! I guess some people just can't handle going without that first cup of coffee in the morning!"

"Well, that's it from us. Goodnight."

INTRODUCTION

If a study has run, with no one around to hear about it, did it still happen?

WHAT IS THIS BOOK ABOUT, WHY IS THE TOPIC SO IMPORTANT, AND WHAT DOES BUY-IN MEAN?

twitter 🐦
Jotbot

If you do not care about what you do, it would be very hard to do a good job.

What is this book about?

The study was a brilliant piece of work. At least that's what I thought. The product manager and lead engineer were happy when I joined the team. When I talked with them about the study I planned, they seemed interested. We agreed on interviewing 40 people for this study that had a goal of identifying user needs and uncovering current product pain points. The product manager wanted to use the results to help develop a detailed specifications document, which will guide the development team. I planned a study that involved four groups of participants – teenagers, students, high-tech employees, and senior citizens. I prepared a detailed discussion guide, then recruited and scheduled all 40 participants. Some of them were held in our offices and some at users' homes. The product manager and lead engineer did not observe or join any of the interviews. I didn't care so much. I was so excited about this project. When I was done, I sat down to analyze the huge amounts of data. It took me three weeks to complete, and in the end I proudly published a detailed report complete with screenshots, in-context pictures of users, video highlights, quotes, findings, smart insights, and recommendations.

The results collected dust.

I gave a presentation to the entire team, during which the lead engineer and some other team members argued that my data was flawed and that they thought we should develop things other than what I was suggesting. Someone said something about the users that I interviewed and that they were not the right audience. The product manager just sat there and didn't say a word. In the following weeks, the product manager published a specification document and the team began developing the product. The document was not based on my study findings and recommendations – far from it. I heard from someone that the product manager interviewed some people, but I had no idea who, how many, or what questions were asked.

I felt really bad. Actually, a more accurate description is that I was very angry. How could they behave like that? How could this happen? Why did they not follow my recommendations? They were acting like typical product managers and engineers, I thought to myself. They just can't develop empathy toward users. All they care about is what they think.

Did you ever have similar problems? Did you ever work with product managers, engineers, or executives who did not follow your study recommendations?

This book describes a framework, strategies, and techniques for working with stakeholders of user experience (UX) research in a way that ensures their buy-in. The primary motto of this book is that stakeholder buy-in for UX research is attained by making it theirs as much as it is yours. Involving stakeholders throughout the process of planning, execution, analysis, and reporting UX research dramatically increases the chances that they will act upon its results.

Throughout the book, I use the following terms.

- **User experience research.** User experience (UX) research provides insights into the abilities and perspectives of people who use different products and services. It is the discipline that studies people, design, and how they interact with each other to achieve specific goals in different contexts. This book is limited to a rich and comprehensive treatment of user experiences for digital products and services, yet much of the discussion can also be applied to other types of user experiences.

- **A product.** "If you can drop the thing on your leg, it's a product. If you can't, it's a service" (unknown source). I don't make that distinction. When I use the term "product," I refer to desktop applications such as Microsoft Word, websites such as CNN.com, web applications such as Gmail, devices such as an iPhone, and apps such as Flipboard for the iPad. Although this book primarily discusses digital services, I also refer to products such as airplane cockpits, command and control centers of nuclear power plants, trauma patient treatment rooms in hospitals, and automobile interiors.

- **Stakeholders.** A stakeholder in the UX world is a code name for the people with whom UX practitioners work. These are our clients, whether internal or external to our organization. These are the ones who need to believe in what we do, to act upon research results, to fund and sponsor future research. We all have a stake in product development. They have a stake in UX research.

- **Buy-in.** "Consumption," "uptake," "engagement," and "buy-in" are words I use throughout this book to indicate that stakeholders use UX research, believe in it, act upon results, support it, champion it, or evangelize it. These words are not synonyms, yet I use them interchangeably because I believe they are useful in describing how stakeholders relate to UX research.

Why was this book written?

When I meet people who practice UX research, I always ask them the same question. I ask what the top three challenges are that they face at work. Getting stakeholder buy-in for research is usually the first challenge they mention. If it's not first, it is in the top three. People have trouble persuading stakeholders to conduct UX research to begin with. They have difficulties in getting sponsorship and budget for fieldwork. They experience hostility when they try to get their stakeholders to act upon research results.

Many UX research practitioners are frustrated.

USE ONE WORD TO DESCRIBE THE BIGGEST CHALLENGE IN UX

Scott Smith, Cofounder and Usability Consultant, Neo Insight, Canada

Neo Insight analyzed the most frequent challenges mentioned in a discussion in the User Experience group on LinkedIn. We were interested to see the challenges people like us face.

The discussion started with this question: "Can you use *one word* to describe the biggest challenge in UX?" Many people responded. It is a very popular discussion on the User Experience group. The group itself is popular, with dozens of thousands of members.

At the time we made our word cloud, 537 replies had been received. We analyzed the most frequent words in people's responses and removed extraneous comments. Respondents found it difficult to choose just one word to describe their challenge.

The main clusters focus around *user*, *design*, *understanding*, and *time*. These are like headings in the word cloud. In our analysis of the responses, many frequently used words also summarize overall challenges.

The audience and user are at the center of the challenges. In one corner are challenges related to knowing the needs of users. In other corners are challenges related to design, the business, and time. All challenges relate to understanding the user, so it is at the center. Other challenges revolve around it: buy-in, understanding, input to design, and the like.

User Experience professionals have challenging jobs!

Figure 0.1: The biggest challenges for UX people (printed with permission).

When people ask me how a typical workday looks for me, I always say that 50 percent of my time is devoted to research planning, execution, or analysis, and the other 50 percent involves politics. I constantly look for ways to get better buy-in for research. I walk a fine line between joy and frustration. Joy comes from seeing people around me consume research and its results the way I expected them to. Frustration rears its head when others completely ignore or disregard research. I now work for a company that employs many people who do what I do, which is extremely encouraging. I remember the days when I was working in companies where research was not my full-time job. It was challenging to persuade people to sponsor and fund a research project, let alone get them to act upon its results. In many cases, I was not able to influence people to change their perception about the value of UX research. I even quit a job where they did not let me do it full time. I know many practitioners deal with similar challenges as I write these words. I also

Figure 0.2: As seen by (printed with permission from Manu Cornet, www. bonkersworld.net).

know that more and more companies and organizations now have a better understanding and appreciation for design and for research. Monty Python sang, "Always look on the bright side of life" even while being crucified (*Life of Brian*, 1979). I would also like to look on the bright side. I wrote this book to provide people who practice (or would like to practice) user experience research with strategies and techniques for getting their stakeholders' buy-in for research. I hope you use this book to get people to better appreciate research and act upon its results.

Who is this book for?

This book is for UX people who practice usability and UX research, as well as people with other job titles who try to do research as part of another job. It is also for people who try to get others to agree to do any research. The book is written from the perspective of an in-house UX researcher and is also highly relevant for self-employed practitioners and consultants who work in agencies. It is especially directed at UX teams of one and those who face no-time-no-money-for-research situations.

If your job comes with one of the following titles (or a combination thereof), this book is most likely for you:

- User experience researcher
- Usability engineer
- Design researcher
- Product designer
- User interface designer
- User experience designer
- Interaction designer
- Information architect
- User experience practitioner
- Human factors specialist
- Anyone who is doing or trying to do UX research as a part of another job

The structure of this book

This book includes six chapters ordered by the different stages of research projects. Each chapter ends with a useful list of its lessons. These takeaways are practical things you can apply in your workplace today to get better buy-in for UX research.

Chapter 1: If life gives you limes, make mojitos!

(Identifying stakeholders, selling user experience research, and dealing with difficult people and situations)

Chapter 1 describes the different roles of business, engineering, and user experience stakeholders. It looks at their perspective about UX research and identifies ways to deal with difficult people, teams, and organizations. It also discusses strategies for selling the value of UX research and presents the Lean Startup movement, which treats research as the most reasonable thing done by startups.

Chapter 2: Mmm . . . Interesting; so what exactly is it that you want to learn?

(Implementing your great participant interviewing skills on stakeholders; asking good questions, listening, saying the right things, and identifying research opportunities)

Chapter 2 is all about identifying research opportunities by developing empathy with stakeholders. The chapter introduces the most important questions to ask your stakeholders as well as tactics for handling research requests and delaying early methodology discussions. It also discusses ways to become a better listener and thinker.

Chapter 3: If you pick a methodology first, something must be wrong

(Strategies for planning studies with stakeholders and techniques for developing the right research questions)

Chapter 3 calls for detailed planning of UX research with stakeholders. It discusses research plans and how to write ones that stakeholders appreciate, focusing on the most important part of planning studies: defining goals and research questions. The chapter ends with a discussion about selecting and describing methodologies in ways to which stakeholders relate and about the power of injecting quantitative aspects into qualitative studies.

Chapter 4: What's gonna work? teamwork!

(Hands-on techniques for collaborating with and involving stakeholders in research planning, execution, analysis, and reporting)

Chapter 4 introduces ways for teaming up with stakeholders. It describes the different stages in which UX research practitioners collaborate with stakeholders for better buy-in for research results. Collaboration with stakeholders happens when planning studies, recruiting participants, interacting with study participants, and coanalyzing the data collected and when results are reported to others.

Chapter 5: The single biggest problem in communication is the illusion that it has taken place

(Strategies and tools to effectively communicate research results by using reports, presentations, and more cool stuff)

Chapter 5 discusses strategies and tactics for better communication of research results to stakeholders. The chapter goes deeply into writing reports and discusses other forms of communicating results such as presentations, videos, posters, and so on. The chapter ends with a discussion about soft communication skills, such as ways to bring bad news to your team.

Chapter 6: You can't manage what you don't measure

(Signals that indicate research is engaging stakeholders and how you can systematically track success or failure)

Chapter 6 identifies nine signs that research is making an impact on stakeholders, teams, and organizations and describes ways to determine whether it is being used well. It also suggests techniques to track and monitor the impact of research.

Case studies and interviews

The book is supplemented by 45 short case studies contributed by UX research practitioners from all over the world. These case studies demonstrate how these practitioners got buy-in for research they conducted, including helpful insights. In addition, the book is accompanied by 30 videos that are available on the companion website (www.itsourresear.ch). Most of the videos are interviews with UX thought leaders and others who have interesting things to say about getting stakeholder buy-in for research. I interviewed in-house practitioners, consultants, people from the Lean Startup world and from academia, and even a negotiation expert and a complaint psychologist. When an interview is relevant to a certain idea, I included a reference to it. Case studies and videos come from all corners of the world, including Australia, Japan, Israel, Denmark, The Netherlands, Finland, Germany, Italy, Switzerland, the United Kingdom, Ireland, Canada, and the United States. The list of interviewees consists of UX industry greats such as Jared Spool, Kim Goodwin, Cennydd Bowles, Caroline Jarrett, Rolf Molich, Donna Spencer, Giles Colborne, Whitney Hess, and Jeff Sauro. I am confident you'll find these interviews insightful.

QR codes

References to book-related websites and to the videos are provided through QR (Quick Response) codes. A QR code is a two-dimensional barcode that includes information that can be read by some camera-equipped mobile devices. You can scan a code with your mobile device and be delivered straight to a specific web page.

To use a QR code, download and install a QR code reader on your smartphone or tablet computer. It will take you a minute to find an app, download, and install it. After launching the app, point your device's camera to the code and scan it. The code will take you straight to the web page you wanted. For example, this QR code points you to the home page of the companion site for this book.

The companion website

The companion website for the book has several goals:

1. Start a conversation about the topic of the book

2. Complete the book with video interviews

3. Provide educational materials for students and lecturers

4. Provide free materials from the book

5. Provide information about the author's talks, workshops, and appearances

I'd like to start a conversation

Getting stakeholder buy-in for UX research is a moving target. Stakeholders come and go, situations change, you change. Many times, when I thought stakeholders really got it, there came a time when the same people showed that they really didn't. This sort of thing made me want to become a lifelong learner of this topic. And I'd love for you to join the ride. What is working well for you? What do you need help with?

I hope that this book starts a conversation among UX research practitioners. I have started the conversation before and continued it while I was writing this book. I invite you to join me and continue the dialog on the companion website (www. itsourresear.ch), Twitter (@itsourresearch), Google+, and Facebook (Search for the "It's Our Research" page).

You are also more than welcome to contact me directly at tomer@itsourresear.ch.

CHAPTER 1

If life gives you limes, make mojitos!

IDENTIFYING STAKEHOLDERS, SELLING USER EXPERIENCE
RESEARCH, AND DEALING WITH DIFFICULT PEOPLE AND
SITUATIONS

twitter
Joey Marburger

It's hard to convince people that the design, UX, and brand are the cake, but technology is the oven. Electricity is expensive.

Introduction

Yeah, but this study will delay our launch date.

Yeah, but we already know what the problems are.

Yeah, but aren't our designers suppose to know what people need? They are the experts.

Yeah, but we can't learn much from only five participants.

Yeah, but we just want to launch and see if it sticks. We'll fix it later.

Yeah, but we can't pay that much for this.

Yeah, but our product managers already do interviews and look at analytics.

Yeah, but A/B testing gives us all the answers we need.

Yeah, but how statistically significant is a study with five participants?

Yeah, but can't we run a quick study with internal users instead?

Yeah, but research sounds so academic.

Yeah, but Market Research already answered our questions.

(inspired by D'Hertefelt 2000)

To be able to sell UX research to people, one must first know them very well. Knowing people well means you know who they are and what makes them tick. Business, engineering, and UX practitioners all have different priorities and pressures. UX research is not always on top of their list. And that's okay. It doesn't have to be. To sell the value of UX research to people who have a lot on their plate requires one to focus on showing the benefits rather than talking about them. Exposing unaware people to usability testing by inviting them to observe users is a first small – yet key – step in building a relationship that is based on trust, mutual respect, and credibility.

Sometimes research is worth fighting for, and sometimes it isn't, and that's okay too. As a UX research practitioner, you learn in time how to make the decision between fight and flight. Most important, you learn to accept the fact that you can't win every battle and that in many cases, there is not even a need for war. If you perceive your relationship with the people you work with as a journey rather than a constant fight, you'll have a better, more satisfying experience.

This chapter introduces the different stakeholders of UX research and their perspectives on UX research. It will give you tools for dealing with difficult people who do not understand or respect UX research processes and help you better sell the value of what you do. It will also bring up the interesting case of the Lean Startup movement. This movement has captured the hearts and minds of many engineers, entrepreneurs, and garage geeks with UX research. The leaders of this movement (some of them interviewed for this book) successfully promote UX research while their audience listens.

Types of stakeholders

Business, engineering, and UX people are all stakeholders in product development. In the effort to develop products, UX researchers are more closely aligned with some parties. This section identifies the different types of stakeholders in UX research (Figure 1.1).

Business stakeholders

Upper management

When I talk about upper management, I am referring to your CEO, VP R&D, VP of Product Management, the entire executive management group, or any other person in a senior management position in your organization who is, might be, or should be affected by UX research. Thanks to the great design of the iPod, iPhone, and especially the iPad (which is owned by many people in upper management), most of them are by now convinced that design is something that is extremely important

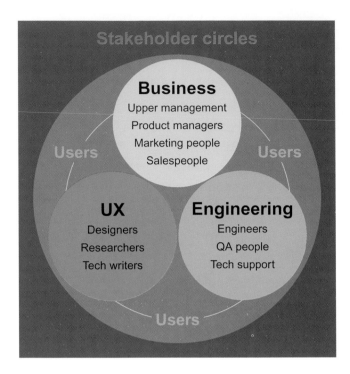

Figure 1.1: Stakeholder circles.

and will try to understand how they can implement design thinking and processes into their organizations.

An upper management stakeholder might take an important role in the success of a user experience research practice. This stakeholder can:

- Provide UX research direction and strategy to key individuals and departments

- Allocate budget to conduct UX research

- Be a champion for UX research by supporting and promoting it

Product managers

A product manager is responsible for many aspects of shipping a product, from identifying target audiences through gathering requirements to developing product roadmaps. A product manager is also someone who is dealing with day-to-day activities such as leading the product development timeline, implementation changes, and priorities. A product manager is usually working closely with many functions in the organization – sales, marketing, engineering (or development), support, and others. Another important aspect of product managers' work is that they usually meet and converse with many customers and users as part of their role in gathering and defining product requirement documents.

In other words – and although it may not seem to be the case in many organizations – a product manager is the center of the product development process. Product management roles are being performed under other job titles such as product owner, business product manager, marketing product manager, program manager, and project manager.

A product manager is a stakeholder who might take the following roles in the success of a user experience research practice:

- Crystallize the connection between business goals and UX research

- Help develop UX research goals

- Provide priorities for UX research based on the team focus and needs

- Characterize research participants

- Participate in drawing conclusions from UX studies

- Help in following through with engineering to make sure that UX research results are implemented

 Many researchers whine to one another about their product managers. Watch my interview with Guy Winch, a psychologist, author of *The Squeaky Wheel* (which examines complaint psychology), speaker, and occasional stand-up comedian. Guy suggests that UX researchers should complain to people who can actually do something about the situation. Otherwise, they will become more frustrated. See the companion website for the full video (use QR code 139 to access the video) as well as a quick summary of the interview and Guy's biography.

Marketing people

Marketing is the process for creating, communicating, and delivering offerings that have value for customers. Marketing people are deeply involved in identifying target customer segments, preferences, and requirements. It is a widely recognized practice and science that spans many concepts and disciplines.

A lot has been written about the relationship, overlap, and tension between marketing and UX research (Jarrett 2000), and cooperation (Swartz 2005). Both research disciplines have their strengths, weaknesses, and quirks. Market research has the goal of uncovering customer segments and customer opinions, and so is complementary to UX research, which mostly focuses on observed behavior of users. This complementary relationship means that there should be many opportunities to work closely with marketing people.

Salespeople

When a company has a sales department, salespeople are the ones who manage the relationship between the company and its clients. They try to understand and meet client needs and try to solve problems and tailor solutions so they can close deals. This work brings them into close contact with upper management, marketing, and product management. When working with and trying to understand salespeople, remember that the success of salespeople is directly related to the success of the organization. Also remember that a salesperson is the company's representative in the client organization and is one of the client's representatives in the company.

A salesperson is a stakeholder who might take the following roles in the success of a user experience research practice:

- Help identify user pain points and delights
- Help understand different user and client profiles and segments
- Support a recruiting effort for UX research studies

As a UX researcher, you have something salespeople might find invaluable: your studies might result in information that salespeople find helpful as a part of their pitch to prospective or existing clients. For example, eye-tracking heat maps tailored for salespeople could be used as a demonstration of how serious the company is when it comes to developing engaging experiences for its customers. Another example for research data that might be helpful for salespeople is data that shows satisfaction levels from your company's product compared to legacy or competitor products.

Engineering stakeholders

Software engineers

Also known as developers or programmers, engineers are the ones who make magic happen. Without them – their thinking, knowledge, creativity, and hard work

– there will be no product. Throughout my career, I've learned a few important things about engineers:

- They want to do a great job in the most efficient way.

- Some of them have a great sense for design.

- Most of them have never observed a user trying to use their product.

- If you don't provide your input on a timely manner, they will not wait for you. I see this point as an extremely positive one because it motivates researchers to come up with research results fast.

As a UX research practitioner, engineers are probably your closest allies. Their logical way of thinking about how to solve problems may not always align with common design principles. If you partner with engineers, you will be able to identify solutions as a team that are better and more balanced than ones UX research or engineering alone can come up with.

Watch my interview with Jay Trimble who founded and leads the User Centered Technology (UCT) Group at NASA Ames Research Center. Jay says it is hard for people who are highly invested in an engineering process to incorporate UX research results into their software development practice. It's always a learning curve. Use QR code 111 to access the video, a quick summary of the interview, and Jay's biography.

Watch my interview with Ben Shneiderman, a professor in the Department of Computer Science and founding director of the Human-Computer Interaction Laboratory at the University of Maryland. Professor Shneiderman says there are still faculty members who think that human-computer interaction (HCI) is not real computer science. He says that only when he was elected to the National Academy of Engineering in 2010 did that change a little bit. Use QR code 133 to access the video, a quick summary of the interview, and Professor Shneiderman's biography.

QA professionals

Very generally speaking, quality assurance (QA) professionals make sure that software products meet certain quality standards through deep involvement in the development process and by carefully crafting and following rigorous acceptance tests.

QA professionals are potentially very close allies with UX research. When you think about evaluative research, such as usability testing, what QA professionals and study participants do has much in common. They both follow a script that describes a real-world scenario and help identify design flaws. Interviewing QA professionals from time to time will help you get a better picture of what works well and what does not work so well in a design of a product.

Technical support professionals

Professional services, technical support, customer care, and call centers are departments in which people are assigned with taking care of customers, their needs, and their challenges. People in those departments have day-to-day interaction with product users and are probably the ones with most customer-facing hours in the entire organization. To a UX researcher, that's an invaluable source of information. A simple thing such as asking tech support once a quarter what are the ten most popular reasons that customers contact them would tremendously help a UX researcher prioritize his or her work.

User experience stakeholders

Designers

Designers are the ones to make products right; they are located on the top of the list of people who need to understand users. Designers integrate business requirements from product managers, user requirements from research, and their knowledge about design into coherent experience creations. Designers have an extremely difficult, challenging job. They put different people's thoughts, opinions, and expectations into one melting pot and create a design that users are expected to be happy with. It's such a hard job that most designers ask for a lot of feedback to make sure they are doing it right. One of the most important pieces of feedback they get comes from product users through UX research. Designers (together with engineers) are your closest allies. They are your partners.

Researchers

Others who do what you do internally and externally look up to you. They are interested in the quality of your research and in how you make an impact with research on your team and product.

Technical writers

Technical writers are involved in three writing activities:

- They create product documentation such as manuals and guides.

- They write product help content.

- They (sometimes) write (or help write) microcontent that appears in products (e.g., labels, annotations, titles, and so on).

Technical writers sometimes need to deal with documenting bad designs. When you partner with them, you are better able to point to problematic product areas to prove or disprove research findings.

Users

Although this book only sometimes discusses users as stakeholders of UX research, they are probably the most important ones. To use a metaphor, you stand on the shoulders of users when you pitch for product direction or design changes following research. You have an implicit commitment to users who participate in UX studies. You must use the data you collect about their behavior and opinion to positively affect product design to their benefit, comfort, and satisfaction. By engaging other stakeholders (primarily, designers, product managers, and engineers), you meet this commitment. In the circle of UX research life, this work makes users happy, which makes UX research stakeholders happy, which makes you happy.

The perspectives of UX research stakeholders

It is key to understand the perspectives of the people we are trying to influence about UX research in general, about specific research methodologies, and about working with practitioners who are probably more interested in psychology than technology. The following is a selection of such perspectives of UX research stakeholders based on the experience of researchers from around the world, as well as interviews I have conducted with stakeholders in the past five years.

"This keeps us honest." I have heard this phrase time and again from many designers and software engineers. After observing a usability study involving their product, they acknowledge the value of usability testing. They understand that now that their product has gone through a true reality check, they have learned about what to keep, what needs fine-tuning, and what should probably be thrown away and redesigned and evaluated. By "keeps us honest," they mean that usability testing weeds out their own opinions and leaves users' behavior to affect the design of the product.

"You are stepping on my toes." In some cases, stakeholders may feel like UX researchers are stepping on their toes. For example, one of the primary roles of a product manager is to gather and define product requirements. One of the ways product managers do that is by meeting or interviewing users and potential users. They are also collecting customer pain points and feature requests. These interviews help product managers create requirement documents. When UX researchers come up with study proposals or results that are targeted at identifying users' needs, product managers feel like someone else is trying to do their job. Without going into debate about whether product managers who feel this way or researchers who come up with these studies are right or wrong, know that certain people may think researchers are stepping on their toes.

"Usability testing is it." When stakeholders are sold on usability testing, they sometimes like it so much that they are not open to any other research methodology that might better answer their question. To these stakeholders, UX research equals usability testing. This is a great validation of past studies, but it often gets in the way of picking the best or most practical research methodology based on the research objective.

"Field research is cool only if it's fast and immediately actionable." When stakeholders are first exposed to a field research proposal, they are usually quick to understand the downside of such research. They realize it's a relatively slow process and that a serious field study usually cannot be completed in a matter of a week or two or three. They also realize, sometime after the study is completed, that results might take some time to become actionable. So the next time a field study comes up, they ask that it be completed quickly and with immediately actionable results. Otherwise, they refuse to support it.

"Negotiate sensibly." The following example from Australia demonstrates a stakeholder perspective about how things should work for users. Research results came in and made it easier for stakeholders to accept a change in preliminary constraints. The reason the UX practitioner was successful here was that he chose to negotiate these constraints in a sensible way without picking a fight.

NEGOTIATING CONSTRAINTS

Gerry Gaffney, Director, Information & Design, Australia

Arbitrary constraints can be particularly frustrating. For example, we may be told at the start of a project that the entry screen must be blue, that everything must be no more than three clicks from some starting point, or that a book can have no more than seven sections.

A client asked me to help redesign a form, but a key constraint was that it needed to be faxable and precisely two pages long. This requirement was embedded in the brief, but an examination of the form quickly revealed that although it used the mandatory two pages, the appearance and flow were so compromised by this physical constraint that it was unlikely that a usable version could be created within the same footprint.

It seemed appropriate to push back against this constraint. The first thing to find out was where it originated. There were two drivers – first, that the form could be easily copied and faxed, and second, that it would not appear daunting to users. It transpired that the first factor was less relevant than it had been in previous years, so it could essentially be put aside.

On the second factor, the project team I worked with was gracious enough to allow me to proceed with design proposals that stepped outside the two-page limit, but with a clear expectation that if the form was considered more daunting than the original version, I could expect to be in some trouble.

Another constraint was that the form should be designed to match the data entry system, which was used to store the information gathered. This requirement was problematic because the system was database-centric rather than user-centric, and a form designed to support this model would be inherently difficult to use. Luckily, the project team was willing to be swayed by an argument that an inconvenience suffered by a small number of data entry staff was a lesser evil than all users of the form suffering.

When the draft form emerged at six pages, I undertook usability testing with a good deal of trepidation. However, users invariably failed to comment on the length of the form and found that the simpler layout and improved flow (many questions applied to few circumstances) was easier. Error rates were also much lower than with the existing form.

Although it's not always easy, I've found that in many cases a well-reasoned open discussion with clients can help remove arbitrary constraints.

The next story, from Israel, demonstrates how an issue of secondary importance (the number of points to include on a scale of survey questions) led to a tense argument between research and marketing departments.

WHAT ABOUT THE ANSWERS?

Moshe Ingel, Usability Expert, Biosense Webster, Israel

During the process of questionnaire design, much of the effort is usually dedicated to the questions. No wonder: question design is a complicated effort that involves decisions regarding the right number, order, and terminology of each question. When thinking about the answers, most people might claim that the best method would be to give respondents a small, even number of options. Our long development process of a complicated medical device includes an external evaluation phase (EE). In an EE, we ask physicians to work with the new product on real cases (treat heart arrhythmia patients) to get feedback and inputs. After each procedure, we ask physicians to fill out a questionnaire to capture their attitudes toward the new product and its features.

In our last version, we had a long debate between the usability expert (me) and the marketing department regarding the number of points on the answer scale. Marketing insisted that four should be the right number; I claimed that nine points are adequate for that kind of questionnaire and users. Marketing had two arguments: one was regulatory (FDA) – we have always used a four-point scale for this kind of questionnaires, and if we change it now, we might need to provide explanations to the FDA about this change. We are not sure we can easily explain the reason. The second argument was about user comprehension and complexity level. Marketing argued that they do not want to confuse respondents with too many options. Fewer options are easier to understand and choose from. The international (United States/Israel) interaction with Marketing went back and forth over both email and phone conferences. Eventually, Marketing "won" this debate (mainly because traditionally EE is a marketing event) and the questionnaire had four-point scales.

During the EE, we noticed that many physicians were marking their answers between the points. For instance, 2.5, 3.5, or even 5. Because Marketing team members observed the physicians fill out the questionnaire, the message was loud and clear: four points are not enough to express the exact attitude toward the new product.

Following these EE events, Marketing (not happily) agreed that a four-point scale was too limited. In the three years since this incident, we have been using seven-point (or nine-point) scales and everybody is happy.

Seeing is believing. The following story makes a point about stakeholders needing to see whether something works with their own eyes. Such stakeholder belief is really great. The design team was smart enough to be fast to react, involve users, and partner with stakeholders.

CHOOSING THE RIGHT DESIGN

Eva Kaniasty, UX Principal, Red Pill UX, LLC, United States

It was an exciting time in the project. We were about to start building a new website. The project involved several highly vocal stakeholders who wanted to be involved at every step and had many opinions about design. In the past, this situation had resulted in tension with the design team, as disagreements over design direction were not an uncommon occurrence. Starting work on a new project gave us the opportunity to start fresh.

The design sessions yielded three viable design approaches and three sketches illustrating them. The approaches differed fundamentally: we called them "the Traditional," "the Fuzzy," and "the Get to the Point." If we let stakeholders decide, we knew they were likely to go with the Traditional – it was the familiar option that would appeal to business-oriented stakeholders. But maybe the more approachable Fuzzy was the answer, or maybe users just wanted to "Get to the Point"? It was clear the users should choose, but who has time to build three prototypes and test them? We certainly didn't.

In the past, usability testing had proven effective in persuading stakeholders to fix usability problems in existing applications. But with a new product, we wanted to harness the persuasive power of usability now, not after time had been wasted fleshing out a potentially erroneous design direction. To the rescue: paper and Balsamiq. Balsamiq, a low-fidelity wireframing tool, allowed us to create three paper prototypes and test them with users in a matter of days. Our fears that a low-fidelity method might not be convincing to stakeholders proved unjustified. It was clear that users were able to engage with the prototypes and give realistic and useful feedback. Stakeholders could see for themselves that for this particular user scenario, the "Get to the Point" option was right.

Because we were able to bring the users' voice into the process at an earlier date, the stakeholders felt convinced that the design direction was rooted in evidence, not just the opinion of the design team. The result? A less contentious design process overall and more stakeholder comfort with design decisions made by the team.

"Did you just say five?" Probably the most frequent question UXers are getting from stakeholders after they realize that a usability study involves only five participants. Stakeholders sometimes cannot understand how five participants (or six, or eight, or twelve, for that matter) can be representative of anything. Some of them gently ask researchers to explain the statistical validity of their findings. Other stakeholders either argue that these studies are not to be trusted, or they just completely ignore the recommendations. The state of mind of stakeholders is to question any finding and recommendation based on very few study participants.

Watch my interview with Meena Kothandaraman, Adjunct Professor at Bentley University and a usability consultant. Meena argues that talking about research in the quantitative language makes stakeholders listen. Use QR code 127 to access the video, a quick summary of the interview, and Meena's biography.

To be able to deal with these arguments, you need to first understand the reason why five is enough. With five users, you are not going to see most of the problems. Rather, you are likely to see most of the obvious problems and a few of the less obvious problems. More specifically, five users are likely to find problems that impact 30 percent or more of users (Sauro 2010). However, after five users, it's less likely that you'll see problems that 10 percent or 5 percent of users will have. In some cases, a problem that affects 10 percent of users can be substantial. You need to be able to understand the limitation, be able to coherently explain it to stakeholders, and tell them that if we want to detect the less obvious problems, we should fix the ones we see after five users, run another five, fix those problems, then run another five (Sauro 2010).

Jakob Nielsen created a famous chart that proves you need to test with only five users (2000). Even Nielsen, in the same column, just a few paragraphs below that chart, advocated for running three rounds of five users, not just five users.

Watch my interview with Jeff Sauro, at Measuring Usability. Jeff says that when stakeholders tell him that five participants are not enough, he tells them they are right. He explains that these will be good only for identifying the obvious problems and that usually, there are many of those to work on. Use QR code 115 to access the video, a quick summary of the interview, and Jeff's biography.

Another elegant way of dealing with stakeholder doubts about the sample size of a study is demonstrated by the following imaginary dialog between a researcher and a stakeholder:

Stakeholder: "Five users? How representative is that?"

Researcher: "What would be a number of study participants you'd be comfortable with?"

Stakeholder: "I'd be comfortable with 50 users."

Researcher: "Perfect; let's go for 50 study participants. If it's okay with you, I'll invite them in groups of five. So first we will have the first five participants, then the next five, and so on, until we reach 50 participants. It would make it easier for me to recruit and schedule them this way. Is that okay with you?"

Stakeholder: "Yes, sure. No problem at all."

Needless to say that after the seventh or eighth participant, stakeholders understand that they don't really need to see more users bump into the same issues over and over again. They ask to stop the study. I learned this technique from a colleague in China (thanks, Xueming!) and it works like magic. Try it out yourself!

The next story, from Japan, demonstrates how one consultancy dealt with objections to usability testing with five participants.

PERSUADING LARGE COMPANIES THAT FIVE IS ENOUGH

Hiroshi Ushioda, Head of User Experience; Susumu Kuriyama, Interaction Designer; Reva Hamon, User Experience International Business Manager, Mitsue-Links, Japan

Our clients and potential clients, especially big companies, often ask us whether five users are sufficient. We have tried explaining the rationale and referencing Jakob Nielsen, but it usually is not persuasive to clients. In general, we believe we lack persuasive materials to convince customers of the value of lab usability testing with few users. But this year, we tried a new method of persuasion and were able to convince a large electronics distributor in Japan to do usability testing for their e-commerce site.

When making the bid for the client, we felt sure that the client wouldn't be persuaded to do lab usability testing with a small number of participants, due to the large number of stakeholders that would be involved in the decision. So we decided to recommend a combination of quantitative research, in the form of remote unmoderated usability testing, and qualitative research, in the form of lab usability testing. Actually, we didn't believe this to be the best plan for the client, because it was much more expensive than they had budgeted for. In spite of that, the project manager told us she loved the bid, due to the quantitative feature. In the end we won the bid, even though the cost of our estimate was by far the highest amongst the bids the client received.

When we finished reporting the results of both tests, the client was so highly satisfied that they decided to continue to do both remote usability testing, and lab usability testing periodically. Many stakeholders, including the company CEO, came to observe lab usability testing, and after watching, they understood the value of qualitative research, even with only a few users. Through the process, the client became a more sophisticated customer and came to understand the advantages and disadvantages of both methods.

In this case, we learned that combining quantitative and qualitative research is a good strategy to use with large customers. As of yet, combining methods is still a lot more expensive than just lab usability testing, so this strategy might not work for clients with smaller budgets. In addition, with smaller clients, there are often fewer decision makers, so it may not be necessary. However, the bigger the company, the more internal decision makers there are in the company. So it is quite difficult to persuade all of them of the value of qualitative research.

Drifting to edge cases. Product managers and software engineers tend to sometimes deal with edge cases. When they do that, they sail into waters that should not be charted. Instead of dealing with 95 percent of the design, they drift to 5 percent and sometimes 0.005 percent of the design. Being a nitpicky person myself, I can understand where this approach is coming from. Their perspective is that the edge case might happen, so we need to think about it and find a good solution to it. The next example shows how one smart UX person managed the focus of a stakeholder.

MANAGING FOCUS, SCOPE, AND PARTICIPATION

Gregg Almquist, Principal, Experient Interactive & Design LLC, United States

While I was at H&R Block working on digital consumer tax products, we created multiple cross-functional teams that were responsible for improving an existing feature or creating a new feature. The cross-functional teams gave us a diverse perspective, and team members across the development organization were able to participate in the design of the product, which built strong team dynamics.

These teams always included a QA tester. Most of them had worked in the H&R Block offices, and they'd seen every tax scenario imaginable. This experience could be really useful as an anecdotal source of information. Occasionally, some of the QA members would propose extensive coverage of just about every scenario they'd ever encountered in the office – even those that were relatively obscure. Once when we were designing a topic, a QA person brought up a scenario we didn't cover extensively. It turned out it was a scenario that had occurred once in this person's many years at H&R Block.

I can't remember the exact scenario, but it was something really obscure – like the child had been raised in a forest by wolves for half the year. I needed to acknowledge the issue – and the contribution – but explain at the same time that if we handled every scenario like this in depth, not only would the majority of the users be heavily overburdened with a more complex experience, but also we would never be able to release an annual tax product. We had to make trade-offs and choices that ultimately helped the majority of our users, the product, and the business. Bringing the focus to these objective success criteria helped move the conversation forward.

> The user experience specialists would often use this strategy, and slowly team members from the other cross-functional groups internalized this point and would raise it when issues of scope creep arose.

"You are very nice. Stay away from me." Some stakeholders perceive UX research as a disturbance to a design and development effort. No matter what you say or do, they will not buy what you have to sell. Here is a story by Michael Summers, who was the only practitioner among all of the contributors for this book who chose to tell a story that does not have a happy ending. Surprisingly, the difficult stakeholder was a designer.

IN SEARCH OF THE USABLE CREATIVE DIRECTOR

Michael Summers, Principal, SUMMERS Consulting LLC, United States

Earlier in my career, I worked at a large agency whose UX team was led by a very talented creative director (CD). Although he enjoyed mentoring younger team members, we always knew that when it came down to a deadline, if the team he'd put together didn't have a really solid comp to bring to the client meeting, he could go into his office for a couple of hours and come out with something great.

I was often in conflict with this guy, but I have to admit that he had fantastic instincts for information design and creating layouts that were scannable and concise. His designs made it easy for users to visually discover which elements of the page or control were needed, and in what sequence – all while juggling the limitations of making sure relevant information was contiguous within a single scroll. He'd walk into meetings with a first draft that was often 80 percent of the way there.

However, the guy just could not deal with the idea that we needed to run real users on designs and then iterate based on the data.

The first few months we worked together, we did a business financing website. It had some complex forms and equities research tools. He put out a fantastic first draft and was then frustrated when I insisted on testing it – with the client observing. We discovered some serious problems involving how users selected individual equities, and pages where users did complex customizations, only to fail to save or enter the changes they had meant to apply.

This CD – we'll call him Greg – went to great lengths not to see what everyone else was seeing through the one-way mirror. On day one, he said the users were the wrong age. So a hasty call to the recruiter resulted in younger traders for day two – same problems. The blocking and denial went on through additional days of research.

I wish Greg's story had a happy ending. Despite more than 40 users in that first study and very tightly edited video highlights of more than 30 users having the exact same problems with that first design, he only grudgingly made any revisions and remained defensive.

He refused to attend the actual findings presentations with the client. As a result, the client had to act as the mediator, taking our findings, working with his team to demand revisions, ferrying them back to us to see if we felt they addressed the problems, and so on. Even when we did follow-up testing on revised designs, he sent his junior folks – if he sent anyone at all.

No doubt you'll go to usability conferences and hear many tactics that are supposed to woo skeptical stakeholders to the lab, like free pizza, heavy use of video, and others. But in Greg's case, he never had the big "a-ha!" moment.

His team would continue to crank out designs that were much stronger than industry average – say, 80 percent of the way there. We would continue to force the issue and have real users interact with the designs and discover important things they'd missed. Clients would continue to observe and realize that if the problems hadn't been caught, they'd lose a lot of money. So they'd lobby for changes. Changes would come grudgingly, and we'd start the process all over again.

I went through it with Greg for over two years. When I moved on to my next job, we shook hands somewhat stiffly and muttered some well wishes. He never really changed his fundamental guiding assumption – which is that UI ought to be created by someone with a fine arts background and that what I was doing was "science" and could potentially kill "the creative process."

I walked away with a stack of reports, video highlights of major problems his first drafts had missed, and notes from clients saying what I was doing was essential.

I guess you can look at it like a Saturday morning cartoon about the "separation of powers." We were like the legislative and executive branches – meant to pull at each other and compromise. But I must say the process isn't super fun. I doubt Greg will ever change. And I know I won't!

Difficult people, teams, and organizations: Fight or flight?

An increasing number of organizations and individuals who develop or offer software products, web applications, websites, and other digital products have a better understanding and appreciation for design, user experience, and research. Since the introduction of several magnificent products and services (smart phones, tablets, web applications, social media, and video games, which many executives now own or use), there has been an even better understanding of what design and research can do to boost a business offering.

That said, it still seems that the majority of organizations and individuals have not bought into the benefits of UX fully – and even less so for UX research. If you encounter these sorts of organizations or individuals, you have a decision to make: fight or flight? To make a good decision, you should start by identifying the maturity of the organization you live in. It might be helpful to do this by considering a UX research maturity model offered here. Several maturity models for human-centered design and usability exist in the literature (Earthy 1998; Nielsen 2006a, 2006b). The following is a UX research maturity model based on the level of buy-in for research combined with the existence of UX research staff within an organization:

1. **Maturity (yes buy-in, yes staff).** The organization believes in and behaves consistently while fully trusting its UX research practice, whether in-house or external.

These are the rare organizations that truly get it. They have deep understanding and appreciation for UX research, and they back it up with action. They ask potential customers all the right questions to understand what they need, and they iterate and validate their designs to perfection. **Fight or flight?** Neither. You won't need to fight and there is no reason to flee. All is good.

2. **Approaching maturity (yes buy-in, no staff).** The organization states that UX research is important, but when it comes to action, there is no staff to act upon policy. The organization might have hired consultants for some ad hoc work in the past and plans to soon hire their first full-time user experience researcher or research team. **Fight or flight?** Neither. This type of organization is currently taking baby steps in the right direction. Join this organization when it hires people or internally transfer to a UX research position if you already work there in a different role.

3. **Approaching immaturity (no buy-in, yes staff).** The organization employs UX research staff but mostly does not buy in to what they do, find, and recommend. This organization is probably the hardest for UX practitioners and researchers. It's extremely frustrating for UXers to work in an environment that sends you contradicting messages. On one hand, the organization appreciates design and research because it allocates headcount and hires the right people. On the other hand, it is evident that there is no appreciation for this discipline. Design decisions are made based on wrong considerations and stakeholders do not cut designers and researchers some slack, not empowering them to do their job. **Fight or flight?** I'd say fight to a limit, then flee.

4. **Immaturity (no buy-in, no staff).** The organization does not believe in UX research (or has no position about it) and does not employ any in-house or external practitioners. This type of organization is probably the easiest to handle. As Frank Costanza once said, "If they don't want me, I don't want them" (*Seinfeld* 1996). These organizations should not (and do not) get the attention of UX people. Maybe some of them will "get it" someday, maybe not. Most chances are that they will. Until then, I believe, it's a waste of time to even try working with them. **Fight or flight?** Neither. You are probably not working for these organizations.

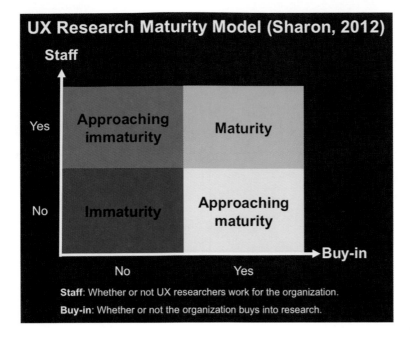

Figure 1.2: UX research maturity model.

 Watch my interview with Rolf Molich, owner and manager at DialogDesign, Denmark. Rolf has a strong principle. He doesn't take assignments on which he does not agree with what the potential client wants to do. Use QR code 125 to access the video, a quick summary of the interview, and Rolf's biography.

 Watch my interview with Whitney Hess, a user experience designer, writer, and consultant from New York. Whitney says that if stakeholders ask to skip research, she understands that they are interested in user interface design, not product strategy and user experience. In this case, she points them to industry UI standards and chooses not to work with them. Use QR code 128 to access the video, a quick summary of the interview, and Whitney's biography.

Many consultants have the privilege of choosing their clients. They can choose whether to work with certain clients and stakeholders. In many other cases, clients that approach consultancies are already persuaded that user-centered design (UCD) is what they need, so consultants do not need to make a big effort of persuading them to buy-in to research. Jared Spool, in his article "Why I Can't Convince Executives to Invest in UX (And Neither Can You)" (2011), and Donna Spencer, in my interview with her (use QR code 120) talk directly to these issues. They don't try to convince the unconvinced.

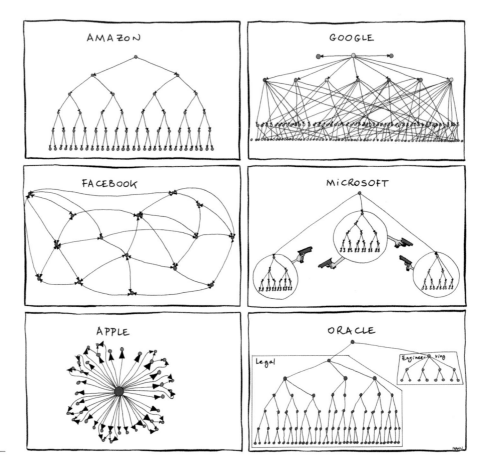

Figure 1.3:
Organizational
charts: how does UX
research fit into these
cultures? (Printed
with permission from
Manu Cornet, www.
bonkersworld.net.)

I definitely acknowledge that there are more situations, complications, and types of organizations. What about organizations that have never believed in UX research and design, never had staff, then suddenly become somewhat interested? What about agencies, consultancies, and self-employed practitioners who deal with organizations that don't give them too many options to fight, just to flight? What about government agencies who follow strict procedures? They may have bought in, but procedures force them to behave in different ways. The world is not as simple as four types of organization maturity.

 Watch my interview with Jared Spool, CEO and founding principal at UIE (User Interface Engineering). Jared claims that there's no point in working with unengaged stakeholders. He suggests that you find better ones. Use QR code 116 to access the video, a quick summary of the interview, and Jared's biography.

My general advice is this: fighting all the time isn't worth it. It can be a rush to join an organization to be an agent of change, but if change is consistently getting blocked, people need to assess carefully whether they want to stay. If you work as an in-house practitioner and you have had enough of trying, you always have the option to join a consultancy or agency. All of the consultants interviewed for this book testified that their clients have already bought into UX and research to begin with and that it is like preaching to the choir. If you choose to work as an in-house practitioner, you sometimes have tough choices to make. Identify your situation and your organization's maturity and make a good, thoughtful call. If you work as a consultant and consider switching to in-house, you need to be aware of the signs for buy-in during your hiring process.

The following stories showcase situations in which UX practitioners could have easily fled. Instead, they insisted on trying, took risks, and succeeded. No guts, no glory.

MORE RESEARCH AS A PERSUASION TECHNIQUE

Richard Buttiglieri, Director of Design, Pearson, United States

Years ago, I was designing a system for call center reps to make referrals to sales reps in other departments within a company. These reps were to get monetary incentives for making the initial referrals as well as if the referral turned into a sale. While conducting field research in order to study the user's workflow, I discovered a number of key factors that would lead to a successful referral, one of which was to support an ongoing dialog between referrer and recipient in the context of a referral. The referrer could learn over time what makes a higher-quality referral likely to purchase and thus receive more money with less effort. This ongoing dialog was the cornerstone of long-term usage of the system because call center reps had very little time between calls for this "other" work.

When designing the interface, I laid out the dialog area in reverse chronological order, as that best supported each user's workflow – to focus only on the most recent response. This was also consistent with other applications the users worked with. The product manager, however, had a different idea: to put the dialog in chronological order because that was how they were most used to seeing a dialog. They fought for "consistency" without appreciating a higher design principle – use the natural order of objects appropriate for the target user.

I tried convincing them with the data I discovered in field research and with a usability test with internal participants that were a close analog for the actual target user. Unfortunately, this did not convince the product manager to overturn his ruling. Because this seemingly small part of the system was so pivotal in encouraging long-term usage, I decided I needed to go bigger – essentially over engineering UX research with several focus groups *plus* individual usability tests of actual end users comparing both designs (in a counterbalanced way, of course). I collected feedback from nearly 50 end users in total and made sure the product manager attended some of the sessions. Only after witnessing the head-to-head comparison with actual end users did the product manager agree that my first design was correct for this situation.

In our field, UCD can mean "user-compromised design," as designers must make design compromises in the name of progress. But when that compromise could potentially put the product's success at risk, it is worth the effort to collect extra data and involve your stakeholders to help make your case.

FOCUS ON PROJECTS THAT PRODUCE TANGIBLE RESULTS

Gregg Almquist, Principal, Experient Interactive & Design LLC, United States

In one of my earliest roles as a user experience specialist, I was often asked to weigh in on projects that were outside the scope of my responsibilities. I believed these opportunities were good for our group's exposure, so I would accept them when time permitted.

One day I got a call to attend a meeting about redesigning the customer support website. Call volume was climbing every year, and the added support costs were negatively impacting the profit and loss (P&L). The company decided to redesign the site in hopes that customers would use this self-service option versus making a call.

The team redesigning the site had no user experience background, but they had a firm plan to move forward, including an information architecture schema. I immediately recognized some basic information architecture and navigation issues, so I weighed in. However, it was clear that my ideas met some resistance because it didn't align with the group's direction.

I decided that our team could knock this project out of the park if we were allowed to lead the design. I contacted an ally of user experience design in the company and explained what I believed we could accomplish if given the opportunity. I laid out a plan – two card sorts to understand how users think about and categorize their problems, a usability study to validate a prototype design, and a review and rewrite of the content. Together we hammered out a budget to hire some contract UX designers, and she got us in front of the project sponsor. The sponsor gave approval, and we were off.

The project was successful beyond our expectations. At the end of the first three months, call volume had decreased significantly, as visits to the support site increased dramatically. Additionally, page views per visit were down, and customer satisfaction with the support website increased nearly 5 percent, which indicated that users were finding answers to their questions with fewer clicks.

This project cemented the credibility of the user experience team's activities and its reputation as a valuable resource for the business.

SHOW, DON'T TELL

Lior Yair, CEO, and Vitaly Mijiritsky, UX Designer, Netcraft, Israel

Our agency was hired to redesign the "My Account" area on the website of one of the largest service providers in Israel, serving well over a third of the local population. Business intelligence data indicated that a very large portion of the requests handled by representatives at overcrowded service centers and overloaded call centers could be solved quickly and efficiently via well-designed self-service online. Our job was to make the interface efficient and enjoyable to use, maximizing the usage of available online services.

We cooperated closely with our client's project manager, coming up with a design that both sides believed in. However, when the design was presented to the executives, they didn't approve it. They felt that it was cumbersome and unclear and that users wouldn't be able to use it well. They suggested a few key changes of their own, undoing our layout and information architecture principles. Our citing of various references from professional literature and similar websites was to no avail, and the final verdict was that it wasn't enough of an improvement on the current interface, and they weren't going to invest significant resources in something that offered "superficial changes" and provided "marginal benefit at best."

Because we were also the ones who were supposed to develop the new interface, this was a big blow for us. After assessing the situation, we decided to go all-in. At our own expense, we developed fully interactive prototypes of both designs, set up our usability lab, recruited participants, and invited the executives to observe the testing with us behind a one-way mirror. We performed a full eye-tracking study, complete with user interviews and retrospective think-aloud sessions. When we saw the executives completely engaged in the process, watching the users' progress, rooting for their own design as if this was a ball game, and listening to the users voice their dilemmas; we knew we had made the right call. Normally, we would also perform statistical analysis of the findings, but in this case it wasn't needed – the executives saw the users handling our design with ease, completing all their tasks quickly and with few mistakes. Their design, on the other hand, brought about a lot of guesswork and frustration, with some participants giving up halfway on several tasks.

A couple of days later, the order came in for the graphical design and the development of our original design.

Selling the value of research

I have seen two approaches to selling the value of research. One involves a conscious decision to not sell research. People who take this approach are convinced that in this day and age, they should not be preaching and evangelizing UX research to stakeholders, prospects, and clients. Instead, they believe, they should only work with stakeholders who "get it." At its core, I support this approach. How much more can we go on and on with saying we are a part of a team, looking for our well-deserved recognition? I also believe that UX research should be evangelized. Yes, we must keep on and on. Change is not something that is easily achieved. Let's look at the filled half of the glass, let's be positive, not grumpy about why people don't listen. Let's sell the value of research instead of almost begging to be heard.

 Watch the fascinating interview with Chris St. Hilaire, author of *27 Powers of Persuasion*, from Los Angeles. Chris defines persuasion as the creation of consensus from conflict or indifference. When done appropriately, persuasion can move mountains. Use QR code 134 to access the video, a quick summary of the interview, and Chris's biography.

The question many people ask themselves is: how best to do this? How does one sell the value of something many others think is redundant? I ask myself this question almost every day. I also ask others in my field how they sell research.

 Watch my interview with Takashi Sasaki, Partner at Infield Design, Japan. Takashi-san says that their pitch to clients who ask to drop the research part of a design project includes a metaphor of a pilot asking to not use a navigation system. Use QR code 121 to access the video, a quick summary of the interview, and Takashi's biography.

Bill Albert also has an interesting answer to the question of how one sells research to stakeholders.

USABILITY IS SUBTRACTION THROUGH ADDITION

Bill Albert, Director, Design and Usability Center, Bentley University, United States

Adding usability to the design and development process both saves time and money. This is counterintuitive to most people, specifically for folks who have not gone through usability testing before. How can you possibly save time by adding a step in the design/development process? The analogy I like to give is asking directions. Sometimes stopping to ask for directions takes a few extra minutes at the beginning but saves a lot of time in the long run. This is especially the case when driving around Boston! Usability testing and user experience research is really no different. Conducting user experience research and usability testing, when done well, clarifies the team's understanding of the users, their current experiences, their needs/desires, and what improvements need to be made to the current design. Without this information, you are designing in the dark. How can a design team possibly know how to design something without this basic information? If they stumble on the right design, it is sheer dumb luck. Much more likely is that the design team comes up with something that isn't right, and it doesn't sit well with the rest of the team. There are countless meetings to come up with the right design, with a lot of guesswork and anecdotes being thrown around. Had the design team only done the upfront research and testing, they would have reached the right design much sooner and with a lot less pain. To some people, testing a product that is going to change doesn't make sense. However, once they see the benefits, they never go back. The old adage "you can pay me now, or pay me later" rings true.

"Research" or "usability testing" sound like big words. People think (sometimes, rightly so) that they cost a lot of money, take a lot of time, and have an academic flair (which in industry might not be a positive thing). Above all, in my view, one of the most challenging arguments against research is that it is perceived as something that asks questions for which people already have answers. Many stakeholders think of themselves as people who know what users need. They claim to have great instincts and intuition about what people want. Some of them are convinced they are users. They use anecdotes from their own lives to prove they are right. Each time I attend a design discussion and I hear the words "I think" or "I as a user," my eyes light up and I pay closer attention. These are the toughest nuts to crack. I see that as a challenge. If people who think this way can be convinced to buy-in to research, I feel I have made the world a better place. I don't fight them. I invite them to come over and observe a usability test.

Usability testing is key to getting buy-in. Many people, including people in the UX world, see usability testing as a low-priority activity that carries little value. And here is a confession of my own. I myself don't really like usability testing. Not because I don't think it's helpful. I think it's *the* most useful thing a development team can do. Personally, I have done so many usability tests that at this point in my career, I prefer conducting other types of studies. That is not to say I don't do them. As a matter of fact, as I am writing these words, I am preparing for a series of six usability tests that I am going to run in a period of ten weeks because this is what my team needs.

If there is one thing I would recommend that researchers do to better sell the value of UX research, it would be to make usability testing a small thing. Many make a big deal out of it. They hire an agency to run a $50 K usability test for them. They have multiple meetings beforehand to negotiate the study, plan, and prepare it. They study eight or twelve people, put about four weeks aside for analysis and report writing, then have a big meeting during which results are presented and a big report is handed out. Yes, there are situations when this is exactly what the organization needs. I understand and accept that. I've even advocated for these types of studies in the past. Today, I feel that the smaller the study, the bigger its impact. If a usability test is not a big deal, stakeholders see it as something they can be involved in. They can be a part of it because they understand it. How do you make a study small? Run one every week or two. Currently, I am running a study once every other Wednesday with three to five participants. Together with the team, we decide what to test on the Monday before the study. We prepare the study on Tuesday and analyze it on Thursday. I don't write a report. Instead, we fill in a spreadsheet with findings and recommendations. The team discusses severities, impact on users, and ease of implementation of each recommendation and decides what will be done when. We then move on to preparing the next study. Recruitment of participants is happening in the background throughout the entire time. This can work if your user population is homogeneous. If not, you can decide that once every three studies you will recruit from a different population and test different content, and so on.

That's how you turn research into a small deal, and that's how I believe you sell the value of research. I have seen many stakeholders "convert" after experiencing and appreciating the value of such small usability tests. After you get this buy-in based on usability testing, you achieve credibility and can suggest other, different methodologies.

To be fair, what I have just described is a practice that is heavily tailored by – and enabled by – the development model used by most of the organizations I worked for. When products are continually updated, research can happen continually. The reality of a lot of release-style software (and other development) organizations might be different, yet there is always a place for not making a usability test a big deal.

THE ART OF SELLING EXPERIENCE DESIGN AND DESIGN THINKING APPROACHES

Silvia C. Zimmermann, Managing Director, Usability.ch, Switzerland

When I started working in the field 17 years ago, I had to write business cases to convince potential clients to embrace Design Thinking approaches in their development life cycle. I had to present them with detailed cost and risk models to demonstrate that they most probably will engage in an unbearable risk when they don't involve their users and clients in their product or service design processes early on. Today, I don't need to do this any more because my long-term clients have achieved a similar maturity model when it comes to usability, UX, and experience design.

One thing that was always very important for me personally, though, was the promise I gave myself when I started working in the field. I don't try to persuade someone at any price. I show them the methods we use, the success we had in other projects, and the importance of embracing UX, but if a client remains skeptical about the added value we can bring to their innovation cycles, then they should not embrace our methods and services. It is not the responsibility of our field to persuade someone that what we do could be beneficial for him or her. That would be the same as if we would try to per-suade someone to stop smoking, if he or she likes to smoke.

Here are my five tips to sell Experience Design and Design Thinking approaches:

1. **Treat your client as a friend.** A UX relationship with a client is like a long-term investment in friendship.

2. **Approach your client with the Design Thinking experience in mind.** Tell your client that you apply UX not just in their projects; make them feel that you approach them in the same way too.

3. **Train your client.** Not everyone knows all the details about all the different methods and processes we use. Always have a small slide deck with nice illustrations with you. This approach allows you to show very quickly the pros and cons of one particular method or UX process.

4. **Be transparent in what you do and plan.** Try to be as clear and transparent as possible: for example, "I select research methods based on ISO 16982," "I evaluate based on ISO 9241," or "I report based on ISO 25062." Doing so helps clients understand pretty quickly what you do and how you do it.

5. **Surprise your client and avoid doing the obvious.** Everyone today knows the basics about UX and Design Thinking. If you can surprise them, you can win them.

To become more successful in selling the value of UX research to stakeholders, you must leverage certain organizational situations. When these situations occur, UX research is probably not in the minds of stakeholders as a discipline that might be helpful. Take that as an opportunity to make an impact.

- **When the organization wants to develop a new product**, offer to help uncover user needs, identify who the users are, their current pain points, and how the organization can add value.

- **When the team plans the next version**, offer UX research to understand what's working well and what can be improved in the current version. Offer to look into the usability of competitor products to better understand their strengths and weaknesses.

- **When the product is about to launch**, lend a hand in planning and instrumenting sensors that will educate the team about user experience success metrics based on usage data.

- **When a new senior decision maker joins the team**, meet with him or her. Show them what you do and highlight the benefits.

- **When a product is succeeding**, propose research to make it even better.

- **When a product is failing**, offer research to help identify the problems and suggest solutions.

 Watch my interview with Dana Chisnell, an independent researcher and consultant at UsabilityWorks. Dana says that when the bottom line changes for the worst, stakeholders become more open to UX research. Use QR code 119 to access the video, a quick summary of the interview, and Dana's biography.

- **When someone is already doing "research,"** use other terminology and find ways to avoid conflict. The following story is an excellent example.

WORDS MATTER

Carol Smith, Lead Consultant, Midwest Research, United States

To gain my client's trust, I try to use clear language and terms and to incorporate the language that they are most comfortable using. In some cases, the client's language supersedes the terms that I would normally use – or even those that would be considered proper.

For example, last year I was planning the redesign of a major website for a client. I needed to communicate my recommendations to the people who would create the clickable prototype. I determined that given the limited time available, it would make the most sense for me to create an initial set of wireframes as a communication tool. However, the people who were to develop the clickable prototype also owned the creation of "wireframes" for the organization. I spoke with the team, and they agreed that my suggestion of making initial wireframes made sense. A win! In order to make the process acceptable to the organization, we had to come up with a different term. Wireframes became pictorial representations.

With another client, despite the presence of a strong and successful UX team within the same building, the marketing department was responsible for "research" and "surveys." The UX team was unable to use those terms to describe any of their work, so common UX methods were hidden with more obscure terminology. A simple focus group became a Joint Application Design (JAD) session, though when we needed to do a JAD session, there was confusion about what to call that to differentiate it as well. The work was interesting and challenging (and most importantly, funded), so the UX team continued to put extra effort into these minor details to avoid major conflicts. I also bring my vocabulary into the client's realm. For instance, I have had a few clients show me their "personas," despite not having conducted much (if any) user research. I take the time to educate them on what a persona entails with regard to user research and plan work to transition the existing documents into true personas. Until that effort is complete, I ask them to differentiate the existing documents by referring to them as profiles or a similar term indicating that it is not yet a persona because it is lacking research to support it.

These may seem like UX "losses," but they don't have to be seen that way. By making the effort to clarify and in some cases change the language we use, the team takes ownership of the work, issues with other teams are avoided, and we can get work done.

 Watch my interview with Professor William Gribbons, Director of the Human Factors in Information Design program and founder of the Design and Usability Center at Bentley University in Waltham, Massachusetts. Professor Gribbons sells the value of research by explaining that it is predicting a problem before it occurs and helps avoid it in the first place. Use QR code 132 to access the video, a quick summary of the interview, and Professor Gribbons's biography.

Perfect your sales pitch. Make sure you come with data and concrete proposals for research. Talk with individual team members first. Get their feedback, change your plans, and get their buy-in. Come to decision makers together. Be approachable, open to other people's ideas. Never give others a feeling you are frustrated. Always be positive. Learn from salespeople. Read books about becoming a better salesperson. My favorite is "The Little Red Book of Selling" (Gitomer 2004).

The Lean Startup movement

Early in 2011 I was exposed to the Lean Startup movement. I had a chance to interview the father of this movement and its most familiar voice, Eric Ries. The interesting thing that attracted me to the principles of the Lean Startup is how similar they are to what people in the UX world have been preaching for decades. The difference is that now stakeholders listen. It's one thing when we UX people talk about how research is important. It's a completely different thing when an entrepreneur such as Eric Ries talks about it.

Watch my interview with Eric Ries, author of *The Lean Startup: How Today's Entrepreneurs Use Continuous Innovation to Create Radically Successful Businesses* and the father of the Lean Startup movement. According to Eric, the Lean Startup approach calls for testing hypotheses. We all agree that we have a strong point of view about what customers ought to want and that we have a rigorous methodology for testing which elements of our vision are brilliant and which are crazy. Use QR code 129 to access the video, a quick summary of the interview, and Eric's biography.

The Lean Startup movement, its literature (Ries 2011; Vlaskovits & Cooper 2010; Blank 2005), and its leaders advocate UX design and research as the solution to their business problems. Eric Ries, a former programmer and current entrepreneur and startup coach, talks about "validation," and Steve Blank, a serial entrepreneur and a Stanford University professor, uses the mantra "get out of the building" (and talk to your users). "Validation" is usability testing. "Get out of the building" is ethnography. This is great music to our UX ears. When I started digging more into the Lean Startup concept, I learned that many startups now want to become lean. They now understand that user experience is a critical aspect of what they do and one of the cornerstones for their future success.

To better understand this phenomenon, here are the principles of the Lean Startup movement based on Eric Ries's approach (2011):

- **Entrepreneurs are everywhere:** As Eric Ries says, "Entrepreneurship is not just about two guys in a garage eating ramen noodles." There are entrepreneurs in many places that you might not expect. Entrepreneurs operate in startups, large companies, nonprofit organizations, and government agencies. All that matters is that you are in an environment in which you create something new under conditions of extreme uncertainty. Many organizations do that.

- **The MVP (minimum viable product):** The minimum thing that needs to be developed to learn whether the product development plan is correct. For example, if your product requires users to download it, develop a single web page that shows a screenshot of a mockup of the product with a short explanation of its benefits, as well as a big Download button. That's it. The next page after clicking that button will either explain why you don't have it or display a 404 (page not found) message. By doing that, you learn how much your product is needed. You created the minimum thing that will help you learn.

- **Validated learning:** Traditional product development follows the waterfall model, in which things work in a linear way and work is passed from one department to another, similar to what happens in manufacturing and product lines. One of the things that happens is what Eric Ries calls "achieving failure": building something that nobody wants, doing it on time, on budget, with high quality, and with beautiful designs. In other words, successfully executing the wrong plan. The Lean Startup approach calls for changing what companies do from "making stuff" to "validated learning." The unit of progress changes from the stuff we make to the stuff we learn to create a sustainable business. In validated learning, teams evaluate their work with real potential customers as a part of the development process. They learn from customers what works well for them and what doesn't and they change what they do to meet their customers' needs. To our UX ears, that's not a big revelation. We call it an "iterative" design process, "usability testing," or the RITE methodology (Rapid Iterative Testing and Evaluation). Use QR code 140 to watch six minutes (minute 23:00 to 29:00) of a talk Eric Ries gave at Google in New York in 2011 to understand how validated learning could have made his life as a startup chief technology officer (CTO) much better. Fascinating stuff.

Watch my interview with Giles Colborne, author of *Simple and Usable*, Managing Director of cxpartners, and former president of the UK Usability Professionals' Association (UPA). According to Giles, stakeholders need to understand why research is happening. We help them understand by framing it as "validation," which answers to their fear of doing the wrong thing. Use QR code 126 to access the video, a quick summary of the interview, and Giles's biography.

- **The pivot:** In an analogy to the basketball "pivot," one foot of a business is always firmly rooted in what we have learned, while the other foot is moving and exploring new changes for the business. If the time taken to pivot is reduced, the belief is that chances of success before funding is gone are increased. Instead of taking the high risks of developing something huge, we make baby steps forward, developing small things and pivoting to better directions. This way, if we fail, the fall will be relatively less painful and allow us to bounce back and continue. On the other hand, if we climbed a big cliff, the potential fall would be deadly.

- **Build-measure-learn:** A feedback loop that incorporates validated learning to make sure the product provides value. One completion of the build-measure-learn cycle is one pivot. You build an MVP, then measure what real people do with it while collecting all kinds of data, and you learn whether your hypotheses were brilliant or crazy.

- **Customer development:** Developing your own understanding of who your customers are and what they are like. This is done through "getting out of the building," interviewing potential customers, observing them in their own environment, and trying to make sense of it. We UX people call it in different names: ethnography, fieldwork, generative, exploratory, discovery research. We create personas.

 Watch my interview with Janice Fraser, an Adaptive Path cofounder and principal of LUXr (Lean UX Residency). Janice is one of the more important voices in the Lean UX approach, which follows the Lean Startup movement. Notice how the following key principles of the Lean UX approach relate to those of the lean startup. Pay attention to the language. There's not a word about usability and user experience.

- A product team includes people who do design, product management, and development.

- Generate many options and decide quickly which to pursue.

- Recognize hypotheses and validate them.

- Rapid think-make-check cycles.

- Research with users is the best source of information.

- Focus on solving the right problem.

- Externalize. Make your work and your process visible to the rest of your team.

Use QR code 130 to access the video, a quick summary of the interview, and Janice's biography.

Silicon Valley has seen many trends and phenomena. Most of them burst into people's lives and went away as quickly as they showed up. Some stuck. Many feel that the Lean Startup movement is here to stay. Here is one piece of evidence to support this belief: Eric Ries's annual conference, the Startup Lessons Learned Conference, was streamed to more than 40 locations worldwide in 2010. In 2011, it was streamed to more than 100 locations worldwide, where entrepreneurs watched it live – in some cases, all night long.

Accept the fact that it might not work and that it's okay

As you know, selling UX research is hard. I attribute most of my gray hair to these efforts. Selling research to people who don't respect or don't understand the value of research is a challenge that might frustrate you. I learned one important thing throughout many successful and not so successful attempts at persuading stakeholders. That thing is to accept the fact that not all people will be persuaded. It is really wonderful and exciting when stakeholders have an "a-ha!" moment. We have all been there. There's no feeling like it. Yet it is not the end of the world if they don't want to buy what you have to sell.

 Watch my interview with Donna Spencer, a freelance information architect, interaction designer, and author of *Card Sorting: Designing Usable Categories*. If Donna hears from a potential client that they want her to do only a design without research, she might not take that job. When she does take the job, she keeps reminding clients that they are making things up, making mistakes, and that they don't know which of the things they do is wrong. Use QR code 120 to access the video, a quick summary of the interview, and Donna's biography.

An emerging theme that came up from the interviews I conducted with UX researchers from all over the world is that you need to develop empathy to UX research stakeholders. UX research is not at the top of their priority list. Sometimes, it is not even on the list. Sometimes they have other, more critical pressures – some of which you might not ever be aware.

 Watch my interview with Caroline Jarrett, an independent usability consultant from the United Kingdom. Caroline emphasizes that the need to develop products that are great for people is only one of the pressures on stakeholders. Use QR code 122 to access the video, a quick summary of the interview, and Caroline's biography.

REFERENCES

Blank, S.G., 2005. The Four Steps to the Epiphany. <Cafepress.com>.

D'Hertefelt, S., 2000. 13 common objections against user requirements analysis, and why you should not believe them. <http://www.interactionarchitect.com/articles/article20000609b.htm> (accessed 09.12.11).

Earthy, J.V., 1998. Usability maturity model: human-centredness scale. IE2016 INUSE Deliverable D5.1.4s. <http://www.idemployee.id.tue.nl/g.w.m.rauterberg/lecturenotes/USability-Maturity-Model%5B1%5D.PDF> (accessed 09.12.11).

Gammill T., (Writer), Pross M., (Writer), Ackerman A., (Director), 1996. The Doll [Television series episode]. In: L. David (Producer), (Ed.), Seinfeld. NBC, New York.

Gitomer, J., 2004. The Little Red Book of Selling. Bard Press, Austin, Tx.

Jarrett, C., 2000. Market research and usability. STC Usability SIG Newsletter, 71. <http://www.stcsig.org/usability/newsletter/0007-marketing.html> (accessed 09.12.11).

Nielsen, J., 2006a. Corporate usability maturity: Stages 1–4. <http://www.useit.com/alertbox/maturity.html> (accessed 09.12.11).

Nielsen, J., 2006b. Corporate usability maturity: Stages 5–8. <http://www.useit.com/alertbox/process_maturity.html> (accessed 09.12.11).

Nielsen, J., 2000. Why you only need to test with five users. <http://www.useit.com/alertbox/20000319.html> (accessed 09.12.11).

Ries, E., 2011. The Lean Startup: How Today's Entrepreneurs Use Continuous Innovation to Create Radically Successful Businesses. Crown Business, New York, NY.

Sauro, J., 2010. Why you only need to test with five users (explained). <http://www.measuringusability.com/five-users.php> (accessed 09.12.11).

Spool, J.M., 2011. Why I can't convince executives to invest in UX (and neither can you). <http://www.uie.com/brainsparks/2011/06/08/why-i-cant-convince-executives-to-invest-in-ux-and-neither-can-you> (accessed 09.12.11).

Swartz, A., 2005. Another usability tool: Marketing. <Usabilitynews.com>. <http://www.serco.com/Images/Another%20Usability%20Tool-%20Marketing%20Sep%2005_tcm3-32533.pdf> (accessed 09.12.11).

Vlaskovits, P., Cooper, B., 2010. The Entrepreneur's Guide to Customer Development: A cheat sheet to The Four Steps to the Epiphany. Cooper-Vlaskovits: Menlo Park, CA.

TAKEAWAYS

In this chapter, we discussed the challenges of selling UX research to stakeholders, who the different UX research stakeholders are, their perspectives about UX research, how to provide value with research, and a primer to the Lean Startup movement. Here are the main things to remember:

1. You closely align with designers and engineers. Many other people in your organization have a stake in UX research. Map them out.

2. Develop empathy toward stakeholders. Understand what they care about.

3. Decide whether to fight or flee from an individual, team, or situation based on the UX research maturity model.

4. Use the driving directions metaphor for explaining why research is important. Asking for directions creates a delay and at the same time makes sure that you'll get to your destination.

5. Invite skeptical stakeholders to watch usability testing sessions.

6. Make usability testing a small, natural thing. The smaller the study, the bigger its impact. When usability testing is not a big deal, stakeholders get involved because they understand it.

7. Run a small usability study once a week or two with three to five participants. Agree on the content of the study with your stakeholders a couple of days in advance. Talk with them after the last participant has left the building. Agree on action items to be completed for the next round.

8. Leverage organizational situations to pitch UX research opportunities.

9. Learn about the Lean Startup and Lean UX movements. Understand how their terminology and practices are gaining traction among entrepreneurs all over the world.

10. Accept the fact that some stakeholders will never understand or respect UX research.

CHAPTER 2

Mmm . . . Interesting; so what exactly is it that you want to learn?

IMPLEMENTING YOUR GREAT PARTICIPANT INTERVIEWING
SKILLS ON STAKEHOLDERS: ASKING GOOD QUESTIONS,
LISTENING, SAYING THE RIGHT THINGS, AND IDENTIFYING
RESEARCH OPPORTUNITIES

 twitter
Joshua Ledwell

Single most important requirement for
successful #ux team is senior managers who
"get it."

Introduction

As someone who studies design and user experience, one of your great skills is interviewing people to understand their behavior, needs, and opinions. Some practitioners out there wear their researcher hat only when they interview users of products and services. Others wear this hat all the time. This chapter demonstrates how to implement your awesome interviewing skills with your stakeholders, especially when you are identifying research opportunities and kicking off research projects.

Other lessons of this chapter are:

- Handling initial study requests
- Asking really good questions
- Delaying methodology discussions
- Saying reasonable things
- Carefully listening to your stakeholders
- Planting the right seeds in your stakeholders' minds

Initiation of a study

UX research begins when either a stakeholder asks for it or a researcher suggests it. When a stakeholder asks you to conduct a study, it is a good sign. It's good because the stakeholder realizes that answers to his or her questions begin forming with the people who will use the product or service. Having said that, I am sure you have received requests for studies that did not make sense to you. Here are several such requests I have gotten:

- [Using usability testing as a sales pitch] Can you go to this prospective client and run a usability test with them? We want to show them we do this kind of stuff to make them want to buy from us.

- [Integrating terminology from marketing research and usability] We need a usability testing focus group.

- [Picking the wrong methodology to answer a legitimate research question] Can you ask a few of our users which features they use mostly?

Sometimes I get different requests, which I deeply appreciate:

- Can you help us prioritize the features we are developing?

- We want to prevent usability problems from happening. We have some sketches we drew on paper. Can we get user feedback on them?

- We are going into a completely new market. Can you help us figure out what people in this market need and how they compare to markets we are already in?

Sometimes I don't get any requests. Sometimes I am the one suggesting that a certain study should be done. I can do that because I constantly listen to my stakeholders. I don't care if they don't invite me to an important meeting once in a while. I proactively search for opportunities to make an impact with user experience research. On the road of converting my understanding that a study is needed into an actual study, I sow seeds by constantly looking around, identifying whom I should talk with, what to ask, and how to listen.

When there is a study request on the table, I immediately ask for a short meeting with the person who requested a study and additional relevant stakeholders and ask a series of very important questions.

The most important questions to ask your stakeholders

People initiate studies for different reasons. The first thing you want to do is set the right expectations with the person who requested a study or wants one (if it was you who suggested it). I cannot stress enough the importance of starting off a study on the right foot. The quality of your study's beginning will have a huge impact on its results. As soon as you understand that there is interest in conducting a study, schedule a 30-minute meeting with your immediate stakeholders. These could be the product manager and the lead software developer, and it's always a good idea to also invite the lead designer and someone from sales.

These people are needed for the following reasons:

- **Product managers:** Because they are aware of the business goals for the product and have a clear understanding of priorities. Product managers can help identify the right audience for the product and the characteristics of study participants. They'll also be leading the development timeline and implementation for any changes that might come up from the study.

- **Software developers:** Because usually they are the ones to be most influenced by research results. They will actually make changes to the code based on study findings.

- **Designers**: Because they are your partners in getting things right. Designers need to understand users in the most profound, deep way, and you need their help in making changes to the design. They probably are also the ones providing you with the wireframes, mockups, or prototypes you'll be using during the study. If the study is more on the generative, discovery side of things, designers are great at capturing critical observations.

- **Salespeople:** Because they are in close relationship with customers and users. Salespeople can help understand the audience for a product and shape the participant criteria for a study. They might also be a critical part of recruiting study participants. The sooner they are aware of a user study, the better they can prepare themselves to help with recruiting.

The meeting you'll be holding should not come as a surprise or as a pop quiz to your stakeholders. Include your short agenda as a part of the calendar invitation. Ask your stakeholders to put some thought into the study and come prepared to discuss it:

Meeting title: UX study prep

Meeting description: Here is a short list of questions that relate to your recent UX study request. During this meeting, we will discuss them briefly.

At this point, when you have an answer, you might be tempted to think about a research methodology that would help close the knowledge gap you are identifying. Try not to think about that just yet. Focus on listening to your stakeholders and on gathering information. You'll think about an appropriate methodology later. Take good notes on the discussion. This step is critical for coming up with accurate research questions.

You might get an answer such as, "We want a usability test because we want to learn whether users like our product." You may be tempted to observe that there are three challenges with this answer:

1. The stakeholder names a research methodology. They ask for a usability test. Best practices are to first define research questions, then match a research methodology that is known to answer these questions.

2. The stakeholder chooses a wrong methodology for their question. The levels at which people like a product or services are not usually determined in a usability test.

3. The stakeholder statement includes a built-in bias. They assume that users like the product and they wish to prove their hypothesis right.

Some researchers might respond to such a stakeholder request by explaining why it is wrong. I would strongly recommend that you don't say a thing about it. The reason is that you are now trying to gather enough information that allows you to come up with a coherent study plan with crystal clear research questions. Your research questions will make the argument for you later.

Timing is everything. The next critical topics to discuss with your stakeholders are time, schedule, and deadlines.

When do you need the results?

To set better expectations, I always ask my stakeholders when the latest time is that they need the study results so they are relevant and effective. The answers I often get might surprise you:

- **Tomorrow.** Bad surprise. In some cases, you can be flexible, but in many cases, you just can't. When you get this answer, it's an indication that the stakeholder doesn't know much about user experience research processes and that you need to put some time on both your calendars to close this gap. Now, don't get me wrong. I'm not saying research can't be done fast. I've sometimes received requests for studies in the morning and provided answers in the evening of the same day after running to the nearest mall to recruit participants for a one-task, ten-minute café study (a low-cost, fast-turnaround usability study usually conducted in cafés, malls, conferences, etc.). Usually, when you provide a fast turnaround, it means that you are cutting some corners. Think about it before you say yes to a "Tomorrow" study. Sometimes cutting corners is perfectly fine. In other cases, it is inappropriate, unacceptable, and plain wrong.

- **Next quarter.** Good surprise. You have lots of time to plan the study, gather great feedback, recruit the right participants, analyze, and communicate the results. Just be careful not to commit to too many "Next quarter" studies for the same quarter. And please don't take me too literally. "Next quarter" means that there is time for you to conduct the study without cutting corners. It might mean you'll be asked to provide results within one month.

- **No idea.** An unknown surprise. This is a trick answer. They might need results next week or next month or next quarter. They just don't know yet. They will know when X happens. Hear them out, but be sure to let them know you might not be available to conduct the study. This kind of reply on your side might make them feel they need to provide a deadline.

The timing issue can bring a whole study project down or change it completely. An A/B test might change to an eye-tracking study or a traditional usability test or a quick café study, depending on the deadline set by stakeholders. In the same way, a field study can turn into a series of in-person, in-depth interviews or phone interviews or a quick survey.

Now for a question that I do not always feel comfortable asking but that I have learned is extremely important: what's going to happen after the study is completed?

What will you do with the research results?

In many cases, as a researcher, you need to make tough decisions and set hard priorities. You also need to decide which team or product needs research love.

Sometimes you are not the one making those decisions, but when you do, you want to be sure you are making the right ones.

One of the most important things to ask stakeholders who request a study is what they are going to do with the results. At first, it might seem like a rhetorical question. Of course we will do something with the results. We are asking for this study, aren't we? Well, it's not that simple, and it's definitely not that clear-cut. Every stakeholder enters a user experience research project with a set of expectations. They expect participants to be able to do this but not that, they expect a certain concept to be less understood than others, or they expect people to have one need rather than another. Now comes research that (hopefully) provides clear answers. They can do this, they don't understand that, and most of them need a feature like this. In many cases, results are in conflict with what stakeholders expected. Some of them realize that their expectations were wrong. Others choose to ignore your findings. This is why you ask this question.

When you ask, "What are you going to do with the results?" you are actually saying, "I might choose not to work with you if you are not eager enough to act upon future study findings." There are two types of answers you might get to this question:

1. "Obviously, we will act upon the findings." It's not a green light, but it's definitely not a red light, either. They might still ignore the findings, but at least they are open to acting on what you find.

2. "Well, it's complicated; it depends on what you find; we'll see." This is not a red light, either, but it's a warning sign. Beware. Sometimes, when I think it is going to help, I immediately reply that in this case I will consider whether I should invest time in this study. They usually change their answer at that point. If they don't or if you choose not to reply aggressively, there's another approach I like to use: I offer to not provide recommendations after the study, only findings. I suggest that we agree together on what should be done about what *we* find during the study. It usually helps. Green light.

Bonus question: What do you know now?

Sometimes stakeholders internalize study findings so well that they think the research was redundant. They say they already knew what it had uncovered. They say they don't understand why research was needed at all. It's an extreme, rare situation that happens mostly with studies that have a goal to uncover user needs and wants. This is a dangerous situation for you, as someone who conducts studies. It is dangerous because it's a signal they won't be asking for your services when they wish to learn about the needs of users. They'll count on what they find, or feel is right, or think is just working, or learn from salespeople. Intuition sometimes works, but not always. You know that in many field studies, you learn about what people really need and don't need. You know that when you visit people at their homes or workplaces, you see things no one can have an intuition about. When I go on a field visit, the first thing I look for is what people hang on the walls that surround them. In many cases, they create things that are missing in the product at stake. When stakeholders say they knew what users need even before the study, it's a sign that you need to do a better job in interviewing them right from the start.

To prevent this situation from happening, you might want to ask your stakeholders one simple question. Because by now you already know what they want to learn during this research project, all you need to do is ask them what they already know. Document their knowledge prior to the study (see Table 2.1). It's as simple as listing the questions they want answered and having them answer them.

- For some questions, they'll just say they don't know the answer and that's why they ask for this study.

- For other questions, they'll try to guess which answers the study will bring.

- And for a few questions, they will have a detailed answer based on their current knowledge. They might give you two answers saying something such as, "Big boss 1 thinks users need X and big boss 2 claims users want Y. We expect

Table 2.1 Documenting stakeholder knowledge in a table prior to a research project.		
Research question	**Stakeholder answer**	**Stakeholder name and role**
How fast do users complete the sign-up process?	"I don't know, that's why we run this study, right?"	Jeff Harrison, Product Manager
	"I'm not sure. I guess users can complete it in 30 seconds."	Laura Bizbi, Lead Engineer
	"My manager thinks users should complete it in 15 seconds, but I heard that the VP of Product Management thinks they should first understand what they sign up for and that they can complete it in 4 minutes. We expect the study results to tell us who is right and what we should do."	Chelsea Bronfman, Sales Analyst

your study results to determine what we should do." That's perfectly fine. You'll probably discover that none of the bosses thought of Z.

After you document what they know and don't know, save this file and put it somewhere you'll be able to find later, if needed. If after you present your findings or even after a field visit, a stakeholder claims she learned nothing because she already knew that, find this file and make smart use of it. I realize you might be asking yourself, "What am I, a divorce lawyer?" No, you're not. You are a person who brings immensely useful information to the organization. This is a smart technique that sets you up for success. And that helps to ensure that people remember your contribution, which is business development for future engagements. Don't act as a divorce lawyer, though. You don't want to be perceived as confrontational. When you have proof that your stakeholders were completely (or even slightly) off prior to the study, make your case in a positive manner. You don't have to be aggressive to make your point. You just want to gently remind them why they asked for this study, what they said they knew before it began, and how different their answers are from what was found. For more discussion about techniques for communicating results, see Chapter 5.

Now that you know the most important questions to ask your stakeholders, let's talk about more techniques and best practices to use during these initial conversations with your team or client.

Delay any discussion about methodologies

At this point in your research project, your stakeholders and you should not be thinking about the research methodology. One of the things that annoys user experience researchers and usability engineers is when their stakeholders ask for a certain methodology prior to putting any thought into what they want to know and why. If you've run a few studies in the past, you probably know what I am talking about. They might ask for a usability test when they actually need a survey. They might want to be really confident with the results while asking you to interview only five users. They might ask for a focus group to test a design. They might also want to show a strategic client who threatens to leave that they care, so they ask you to run a usability study with them. These requests indicate different knowledge levels that your stakeholders have about research methodologies. Your stakeholders' knowledge about methodologies directly affects the words they use when they ask for a study. The more they know, the more specific the request is. You want to gently and respectfully skip that part of their request – especially when they don't have a good grasp of research methodologies. No matter what your stakeholders know or don't know, you want to delay any discussion about research methodologies for two reasons:

1. **It's your job.** Matching research goals and questions with a methodology that brings valid and reliable results is a skill researchers have, or should have. With all due respect to engineers, product managers, and marketers, it takes a lot of reading, training, and experience to become good at this. Yes, I know many user experience practitioners do not have formal education in HCI or psychology. Heck, until ten years into my career as a researcher, I didn't have any. I am also aware that many practitioners don't have much experience. When you think about it, even Jakob Nielsen, Jared Spool, and Alan Cooper started somewhere. In the first two or three years of their careers, they also didn't have much experience. You get experience by conducting studies. When you don't have the formal educational kosher stamp or when you don't have much experience, I suggest that you read. A lot. A lot more than what your stakeholders might read about user experience research and design. Even if you do have a formal stamp, keep reading. UX is broad, and it is a hallmark of a good practitioner to be well read. All these forms of learning, individually and combined, will help you match a goal with a methodology. You do not write code, nor do you persuade prospects to purchase products. This is your job. You are a user experience professional. This is what *you* do.

2. **You need time to think.** Sometimes it is pretty straightforward to match a research question with a methodology. But in many cases it isn't, even though it might seem easy. I think experience is really important here – primarily other people's experience. You want to think about the methodology that will provide answers to your stakeholders. You want to be right. You want to take advantage of others (in a good way) and consult with experienced people. The one great thing about the user experience community is that it is extremely supportive, available, and willing to help you. One of the most useful resources is a secret, online list that cannot be mentioned here (contact me at tomer@ itsourresear.ch if you want details). Use it. My point is that the process takes time and a lot of thought needs to be put here.

One of the most important things you need to do is to align your stakeholders with you, and what will eventually help you delay discussions about methodologies is saying reasonable things.

Become the voice of reason

What you communicate to your stakeholders when they first ask for a study has an enormous effect on the end result. In other words, what you say now determines the level of impact of the study. Yes, it is that dramatic. When you communicate, there's the text that comes out of your mouth, documents, or emails. There's body language that (in most cases) unwillingly takes care of what you really think and don't want to say. And then there's subtext, which includes things that are implied by what you say or do. Your job is to control all of these communication channels so that they communicate one message to your stakeholders: I'm here to help us do a better job. This message means that you know what you are doing and that you are a confident professional.

Your communication now affects the end result of the study because it sets both the atmosphere and the expectations of your stakeholders. By atmosphere, I refer to issues such as:

- Does the team trust the researcher to bring useful results?

- Is there mutual respect between stakeholders and the researcher?

- Does the researcher think this study is right or that the request is legit?

- Is everyone excited with the study or are there any dark clouds over it (maybe a nonsupportive executive)?

As for expectations, I could not stress enough the importance of setting the right expectations. Imagine what might happen if any one of the following occurred in the end of a study:

- Your product manager says he needed the results three weeks ago.

- Engineers complain that study participants were not representative and that there were not enough of them.

- The VP of sales was heard saying that user research does not give any added value. Salespeople, she said, could have provided similar insights about client needs.

Although you cannot prevent people from drawing these types of conclusions, you can minimize the chances of this happening if you make sure the right expectations for studies are clearly defined, understood, agreed upon, and met. Becoming the voice of reason means, among other things, that you make sure you set the right atmosphere and expectations.

How else can you become the voice of reason? At this point, when you are trying to learn as much as you can about a possible user experience project, you primarily want to ask good questions. Being a professional means that you do not express your opinions about what needs to be done – not just yet. What you should do now is make sure you have all the information you need to decide whether you are going to propose a research project and what this project is going to include.

One of the best examples I have for showing your stakeholders that you are the voice of reason relates to the words you use that indicate who owns the study. You can easily hear your product manager saying something like, "So, when do you think you can share a written plan for your study?" The instinct would be to answer their question, but that is the wrong response. The language that you and your stakeholders use is important. It's not *your* study. It's theirs and yours. Don't let anyone, including you, refer to it as his or hers. It's not about any of you. It's about what the study reveals and what the results tell about how products can be better. When a stakeholder says something like this to me, I immediately stop the discussion and very clearly explain that it is not my study, it's ours. I do it with a smile, not aggressively. By using language to imply shared ownership, I communicate that this matter is important.

Listening and sowing seeds

If I needed to summarize this section in one sentence, I'd say *shut up, listen, then start talking.*

User experience practitioners who are also excellent interviewers know that listening is a key aspect of a successful interview. How many times have you found yourself wondering, "Did I just say that?" Sometimes a word, a gesture, or even a blink or a certain body posture can bias an interviewee and add flaws to data you collect. Let's discuss several aspects of listening to your stakeholders. You will quickly see how these are similar to techniques you apply when interviewing users.

Take notes. When you listen to what stakeholders say, take accurate notes. You will find these notes extremely useful when you move on to creating the research plan, especially when you phrase research questions and participant characteristics. Taking notes also shows your stakeholders that you care about what they think and want. It's all about respecting each other. I once had a study participant who noticed that I stopped typing on my laptop keyboard and immediately responded, "That's it? I'm not saying anything important any longer?" Your stakeholders are no different.

Do not interrupt. An additional way to show disrespect to your stakeholders is to keep interrupting them as they answer your questions and express their thoughts. When you truly listen to a person you converse with, you have no reason to interrupt them. Some people, when interrupted, tend to lose their line of thought, so you might also be missing important information.

Encourage a conversation. When there are several stakeholders you meet with, it's a golden opportunity for codiscovery. When you ask a question, try creating a conversation between stakeholders. It will help you understand the sometimes many aspects and layers of answers. It might also uncover hidden political forces and tensions you were not aware of and that might affect the future of the study and its impact.

Ask open-ended questions. When you ask your product manager, "Do you want me to invite 30- to 40-year-old women for this study?" you've invited them to say, "yes" or "no." What you really want to know is why. Instead, try this open-ended phrasing: "Tell me about the participants you want to see in this study."

Look for body language signals. By the body language signals your stakeholders give you, you can tell if they truly want the study they are asking for, if they are forced to ask for it, if they are interested in the results, what they think of you and your ability to help them, and much more. Very generally speaking, if you see your stakeholders sitting back, crossing their arms and legs, and not looking you in the eye, you have a challenge ahead of you. If they sit up straight, maybe at the edge of their chair, lean forward, and wave their hands when they talk, you can tell that they are engaged, excited, eager to partner with you, and open to learning from users.

Don't ask leading questions. You want to ask the most neutral questions, not bias your stakeholders. When you ask nonleading questions, your stakeholders talk more, give you more helpful information, and allow you to listen.

Don't think too much. You are now in information-gathering mode. Think army intelligence. You don't plan your moves now. You don't think about the data in front of you. All you do now is collect and gather. Later on, you'll think about it. If you think now, you don't listen.

 Watch my interview with Donna Tedesco, a Staff Usability Specialist in the user experience research team at a large organization located in Boston, Massachusetts. Donna talks about how she identifies research opportunities in her organization. Use QR code 114 to access the video, a quick summary of the interview, and Donna's biography.

In order for you to truly affect people, teams, organizations, and products with user experience research, you need to not only listen but also talk, but not too much. It's about quality, not quantity. When you hear a version of the same thing repeated in three different meetings by several stakeholders, use it. The next time you meet one of these stakeholders – or, even better, his or her manager – mention it to them. Say something such as, "I've been hearing that information about X has become a knowledge gap in our team. What do you think? Do you think it can be filled in with input from user research?"

Another way to sow seeds is repetition. It works for politicians and children. Politicians believe that if their message is repeated countless times, their voters (and potential voters) will eventually think it's true or right. Children also need to experience something again and again to become satisfied. And then they want to experience it once again. Bottom line: repeat your message like a broken record. When you hear your stakeholders repeat what you have been consistently saying, it's a sign that you planted the right seeds. Let's say you've identified an opportunity for making an impact with user experience research. Create some kind of a mantra – a phrase that you keep using each time something relevant is being said in a meeting or conversation. For example, let's say that you've determined that the team doesn't know anything about what users do with information they export from the product. Do they import it into Microsoft Excel? Do they print it and hang it on the wall? Why do they export information? You listened well and kept hearing stakeholders and their managers refer to this knowledge gap. The mantra you might use each time someone mentions that they don't know what users export and why would be: "Watching a few users export data is easy; we could do it next week." Repeat it at every (relevant) opportunity. Eventually, it will sink in. When you hear the product manager saying that watching users export data is easy and can be done next week, it's a sign that you've done well.

 Watch my interview with Paul Adams, a product manager at Facebook. Paul, previously a UX researcher, talks about the pressures and priorities product managers have. Use QR code 112 to access the video, a quick summary of the interview, and Paul's biography.

TAKEAWAYS

This chapter focused on interviewing your stakeholders at the beginning of a user experience research project. Here are the main points to remember:

1. Getting requests to conduct research is a good thing. Not getting any requests should concern you.

2. Kicking off a research project with a short meeting, during which you ask your stakeholders the following questions, is key to the success of the study:

   - What is the product?

   - Who are its users?

   - What do you want to know? Why?

   - When do you need the results?

   - What will you do with the results?

   - Bonus question: What do you know now?

3. Push back attempts to affect the methodology selected for the study before a study plan is ready. Matching a methodology to research questions takes some thought and doing so is your job, not your stakeholders'.

4. Words you use determine the level of impact the study will have. Use them wisely.

5. Set reasonable expectations among your stakeholders. Be honest and straightforward.

6. When you interview your stakeholders, be quiet and listen very carefully to what they have to say.

7. Use these great interviewing techniques: take notes, do not interrupt, encourage a conversation, ask open-ended questions, look for body language signals, don't ask leading questions, and don't overthink about the answers.

8. Attend your stakeholder meetings and try to identify knowledge gaps related to users, their needs, and their experience.

9. When you identify a knowledge gap, repeat the fact that it exists, hoping that someone will suggest conducting research to fill the gap.

CHAPTER 3

If you pick a methodology first, something must be wrong

STRATEGIES FOR PLANNING STUDIES WITH STAKEHOLDERS AND TECHNIQUES FOR DEVELOPING THE RIGHT RESEARCH QUESTIONS

twitter
TK

Even with all the technology in the world, nothing beats two people huddled around a whiteboard.

Introduction

Different researchers and teams have different study planning strategies. Some go through very light planning, mostly orally. Other researchers extensively plan and document every detail; some would say they overplan. Regardless of your planning strategy, I would argue two things: that you must partner with your stakeholders when planning, and that you must be able to boil your plan down to a one-page description. The most important part of this plan is the list of research questions: the specifics of what you are after, supported by a well-defined goal. An additional key aspect of the plan is the methodology, which you and your stakeholders get to only after the goal and questions are defined. In this chapter, you will find discussions about writing research plans, defining study goals, and crafting research questions with your stakeholders. Finally, I'll recommend one great idea you can use to engage stakeholders while planning (and later, when study results are in) – adding a quantitative aspect to your qualitative study in the form of key metrics that you plan to collect and use to measure success.

Research plans

Research plans are documents that serve as blueprints for research projects. They are an important tool for setting stakeholder expectations of research and present a great opportunity to collaborate with your team. They usually include the following sections (note that later in this chapter I provide a sample one-page plan):

1. **Background:** a short description of the status of the product or project that led to planning this study.

2. **Study goal:** the high-level reason for conducting the study and what success looks like.

3. **Research questions:** a list of questions to be answered during the study. Research questions are a translation of the study goals into operational specifications that drive the design of the study.

4. **Methodology:** a description of the way research questions are going to be answered.

5. **Participants:** the characteristics of the people who will be invited to participate in the study.

6. **Schedule:** due dates for key study activities: participant recruiting, actual study, and results publication.

There are many variations of research plan contents in terms of sections, length, level of detail, format, and audience. The following are examples of research plan variations:

- **Sections:** in addition to the sections described earlier, sometimes it's important to include additional sections such as "Analysis plan," "Final report content," and "Recruiting plan." The sections you include should be based on your research goals and stakeholders; there's probably no right or wrong approach.

- **Length and detail:** some plans are extremely short, some are quite lengthy. Short plans might include only the goal and questions that the study is trying to meet and answer. Longer plans might include a detailed session agenda, script, and detailed specifications of study setup and technology usage.

- **Format:** plans might take form in an email message, document, or presentation. I find the format to be a less important issue, although my experience shows that a document is the most positively received format to communicate a plan.

- **Audience:** different audiences require different research plan contents. A plan prepared for an audience new to user experience processes will be different than a plan for a more UX-savvy audience. People new to UX probably can handle less jargon (which is recommend in many cases) and need more details in plain language when describing the process.

I'm a big fan of planning, and I am aware that there are practitioners with different preferences in regard to writing research plans. Next, I'll discuss several such preferences. We'll try to figure out who the users of study plans are, what they want, and what they need. Later, I'll discuss three planning practices: long plans, no plans, and – my stakeholders' preference – very short plans.

Users and purposes of study plans

Research plans serve several purposes. The first is providing a blueprint for the planned research activity. Plans help set a common language between all involved parties, and they are a tool for reassuring stakeholders that what was agreed upon during initial conversations is in fact what is going to happen.

When you suspect that people are too busy to read research plans, I suggest you schedule a meeting with a goal to make immediate stakeholders aware of the study plan and to gather their feedback. In some cases, you will need them to sign off on a plan to make sure that you are covered in case they change their minds (I must admit that I've never done this, but I am aware of such situations). In any case, use this opportunity to involve everyone in setting the plan for the study. Carefully listen to criticism and ideas different than yours to learn more about what stakeholders expect to get from the study.

 Watch my interview with Donna Tedesco, a Staff Usability Specialist in the user experience research team at a large organization located in Boston. Donna tells a story about what happened when a stakeholder did not attend a planning meeting of a study. Use QR code 114 to access the video, a quick summary of the interview, and Donna's biography.

Keep in mind that different stakeholders might be interested in different aspects of a research plan:

- **Product managers and software developers** will mostly be interested in the goal, research questions, and schedule. In some cases, they will also be interested in participant criteria, but not always. These stakeholders are usually interested in goals and questions because these determine the content of the study and its focus. They will also be interested in the schedule to make sure that it meets their needs for making timely design, business, and development decisions. Participant criteria will interest them if they are targeting a very specific audience and they want to make sure that study participants are representing this audience as much as possible.

- **Designers** are your closest allies. They will probably show interest in the entire plan because they are probably the stakeholders who are most affected by the results of the study. They are the ones who probably need to create something or make changes based on the results.

- **Salespeople** will be interested in participant criteria because this will affect their level of involvement in the process of recruiting participants for the study.

- **Executives** will probably be interested in the study goal and in the overall cost of the study, as they are likely sponsoring the study. Usually, their bandwidth does not allow them more than that.

- **Other UX researchers** internal and external to your organization might be interested in your plan for two good reasons. First, they might be coleading a study with you. It is critical that all leaders be on the same page at the start of the study. For instance, a study with coleaders in different countries is vulnerable to chaos and lost time if the goal is not stated precisely and checked to see that the translation hasn't changed the meaning. Second, other researchers might want to learn from you. Many plans that I read help me shape better plans for my own studies.

- **You!** The plan is mostly for you. As soon as you put your thoughts in writing, something happens, and you find holes in them. These holes you find help you improve your plan. A written plan also helps you focus and better prepare for the study. The fact of the matter is that if you can't boil your plan down to a single page, it means that you yourself probably don't really understand it.

One thing you might ask yourself is when the best time is to share a plan with stakeholders. I'd say early and often. Share a plan when you have only draft goals and research questions. Share it when you have a final list of goals and questions. Share it again when you've selected a methodology. You see where I'm going with this. It's a bad sign when your stakeholders are surprised by the content of a study plan.

 Watch my interview with Jay Trimble who founded and leads the User Centered Technology (UCT) Group at NASA Ames Research Center. Jay claims that Microsoft PowerPoint presentations and explanations will not help stakeholders "get" user experience research. They will get it only with experience. He recommends involving them in planning research and asking them questions about what they want to know. Use QR code 111 to access the video, a quick summary of the interview, and Jay's biography.

Now that you have an idea of who needs plans, when, and why, let's discuss something that I believe is a critical factor in getting stakeholders to work with you on a research plan: the plan's length.

Long plans

Long plans are not necessarily a bad thing. Nowadays, people have short attention spans and many tend to not read long documents. Nonetheless, long plans are sometimes vital. I can easily imagine situations in which safety is an issue during a study. When that is the case, I as a stakeholder or external client would require detailed specifications about the safety of participants, moderators, and observers. These details might mean that the planning document is lengthy. Another good reason for a long plan occurs when the study script or protocol is also required and included in the document.

Sometimes plans become long for the wrong reasons, such as extremely long lists of research questions. I have seen plans with 50 research questions. I can't really see a situation in which that size of a list is useful to anyone for a single study. Another wrong reason is extra, redundant, and unneeded wording . . . if you see what I mean.

In many situations, a plan is long because extra and noncritical sections are written. These sections should probably be left out of the initial plan. Remember, your goal is to attract stakeholders to read, engage, and work with you on the plan. The following are sections that might be making a research plan too long:

- **Detailed methodology.** Yes, it's sometimes needed, but in many cases you are the only one who understands what's in this section. If that's the case, specify the methodology in a separate document and provide only the highlights in the plan you share with stakeholders.

- **Team assignments.** I know, I know. It's important that everyone knows what he or she needs to do before, during, and after the study. Personally, I prefer email for such assignments. Do not pollute the plan with to-do lists.

- **Script (or study protocol).** A study plan is a living document. When it is first shared with stakeholders, it should be short. That is why my plans always include a script section entitled, "Script (TBD)." (TBD stands for "To be determined.") I do this because I want my stakeholders to know that the script will be added to the plan and that this is the document they will need to access to read it. Another way to keep the plan from becoming a tome is creating a separate document for the script.

- **Analysis plan.** In many cases, an analysis plan is not important to have or to communicate to the team. I don't see why you need one for a traditional, formative lab usability study. Sometimes an analysis plan might become relevant. For example, when you have a quantitative component to your research, it is important to define what you will do with various measurements and how they will be used to support findings.

- **Educational pieces.** Sometimes you wish to educate your team and stakeholders about user experience and usability. You want to teach them about the benefits of the methodology you selected, or about the study environment, or about how you create rapport with study participants. These are noble goals I cannot argue with. I do have a problem with the format. I would argue that UX education should be embedded in other formats. For example, if you have the luxury of working with another UX researcher, you can use valuable observation room moments to educate stakeholders.

You get the point. There are many reasons to have a long plan. There are also many great reasons for having short plans. Of course, there's another option, which is a combination of the two; write a long plan with a leading executive summary so it becomes a short plan for those who want to only read the summary. Have a good reason for including each and every section in the plan. And if you must include a section, that's okay. Just make sure that it communicates what's important in the shortest way possible.

Some UX practitioners choose not to write study plans at all. The next section discusses why this might be a good or bad idea.

No plans

Sometimes researchers have no plans. Or they have plans, but they choose to keep them in their heads rather than having written plans. Some people can freak out just hearing about the idea of not having a written plan. Some don't understand what the fuss is all about. Of course, I can discuss good reasons for not having written research plans. And I will in a moment. My point is that you should look at it from the perspective of your stakeholders. Do they need a plan? Will they be more engaged with and bought into the study, the findings, and recommendation if you have or don't have a plan? A plan might be acceptable for one stakeholder and not for another. It could be acceptable by a single stakeholder at one point in time, and not in another. In Chapter 2, I discussed ways to plant the right seeds in your stakeholders' minds. Having a written plan is one of those seeds you must sow. A plan helps you get a better feel for your stakeholders and identify what works and doesn't work well for them. Researchers need to be very conscious of their customers and to ensure that they are properly engaged in the plan. If there's no written plan, they're unlikely to be engaged.

 Watch my interview with Rolf Molich, owner and manager at DialogDesign, Denmark. Rolf is very opinionated about treating our stakeholders as our users and about how we experts need to swallow our own medicine by ensuring that our communication, such as a study plan, is highly usable. Use QR code 125 to access the video, a quick summary of the interview, and Rolf's biography.

Here are some reasons for not having a written study plan:

- **Everybody is already aligned.** A very good reason to not have a study plan is when stakeholders are so used to UX research going on that they don't need yet another document. When you agree to have a "lab study to improve the usability of feature X," everybody knows what this means. They know it because they were deeply involved in past lab studies and because you were deeply involved in the development process. Trust is key here. You trust them to know what to expect from a lab study and they trust you to know enough about feature X to design a relevant study.

- **Save time.** Some plans are not written because researchers believe that writing them would take up time they don't have. They might think that stakeholders appreciate them spending time on actual "face time" with users instead of document-writing time.

- **Avoid debate by keeping plans vague.** Certain people like to argue about everything. You know these people. Some of your stakeholders might be those people.

Developing a research plan with opinionated stakeholders and the fact that actual customers (or potential customers) are involved often results in heated debates. In some cultures, heated debates mean angry faces and long silent moments. In other cultures, they might mean yelling and slamming doors. In any case, one can understand why researchers sometimes want to keep plans vague and avoid debates.

- **The study is a part of a master study program.** Sometimes there is a master research plan that defines overall goals in addition to research milestones to achieve these goals. If this master plan is detailed enough, there might not be a need for a separate plan on every single study.

Despite these arguments, the bottom line is that you should always have a written study plan, even if you don't share it with anyone else. When you put things in writing, they look very different compared to how you imagined them when they were just thoughts inside your head.

The next section discusses the plan format that I've found works best for stakeholders and for me: the one-page plan.

The plan stakeholders love: The one-page plan

These are the sections included in a one-page research plan (or in an executive summary of a long plan). I found that stakeholders love brevity and appreciate succinct definitions of what's going to happen, why, when, and with whom. See Table 3.1 for a a sample one-page research plan.

Title. The title should state a combination of the thing you study and the methodology: for example, "Monster.com field study" or "xyzPhone data entry usability testing." Sometimes it's also appropriate to include some kind of an indication about the target audience for this study. For example, "Whitehouse.com news page interviews with senior citizens."

Author and stakeholders. Add your full name, title, and email address in one line. After you get your stakeholders' buy-in for the plan, add their names as well.

Date. Update it whenever the plan is, well, updated.

Background. Briefly describe what led to this study. Discuss the short-term history of the project. Be concise: no more than five lines.

Goals. Briefly state the high-level reason (or reasons) for conducting this study. I'd make an effort to phrase it in one sentence. If it doesn't make sense, create a numbered list of very short goal statements. If you have more than three or four goals, you are either aiming too high (meaning that you have too many goals) or you are repeating yourself.

Research questions. These are the specifics – the core of your plan. Provide a numbered list of questions you will answer during the study. It is extremely important that your stakeholders understand that these are not necessarily questions you will ask study participants. As a ballpark estimate, you should probably have no more than seven to ten questions, preferably around five questions. Another important aspect of stating the research questions is that they will help you when you write the study script. You will construct your script trying to answer these questions.

Methodology. In an academic environment, this section has one primary goal: to provide as many details as are necessary for another researcher to be able to repeat the exact same study. In practice, the goal of the methodology section is to succinctly inform your stakeholders about what is going to happen, for how long, and where.

Participants. Provide a list of the primary characteristics of the people you will recruit to participate in the study. Make sure you have a good reason for each and every characteristic. If you have two participant groups, describe both groups' characteristics in lists or in a table. Add a reference to a draft screener with which you'll recruit study participants.

Schedule. Inform stakeholders about at least these three important dates: when participant recruiting starts, when the study is happening, and when they can expect to get results. Large research efforts require more scheduling details. For example, if the study involves travel to another city or country, it might require adding more important dates such as onsite preparation and meetings or dates for analysis workshops.

Script placeholder. When a full study script is ready, it will appear under this title. Until then, all you need is a title with a TBD indication.

Table 3.1 A sample one-page research plan

xyzPhone data entry usability test

By John Smith-Kline, Usability Researcher, jskline@iphone.com

Stakeholders: Wanda Verdi (PM), Sam Crouch (Lead Engineer)

Last updated: February 1, 2012

Background

Since January 2009 when the xyzPhone was introduced to the world, specifically after its market release, journalists, bloggers, industry experts, other stakeholders, and customers have privately and publicly expressed negative opinions about the xyzPhone keyboard. These views suggested that the keyboard is hard to use and that it imposes a bad user experience for customers. Some claimed this is the main reason the xyzPhone will not be successful among business users. Throughout the years, several improvements were made to data entry (such as using horizontal keyboards for most features), to no avail.

Goals

Identify the strengths and weaknesses of data entry in the xyzPhone and provide opportunities for improvement.

Research questions

1. How do people enter data to the xyzPhone?

2. What is the learning curve of new xyzPhone users when they enter data?

3. What are the most common errors users make when they enter data?

Methodology

A usability study will be held in our lab with 20 participants. Each participant session will last 60 minutes and will include a short brief, interview, task performance with a xyzPhone, and a debrief. Among the tasks: enter an email subject heading, compose a long email, check current news updates at CNN's website, create a calendar event, and more.

Participants

These are the primary characteristics of study participants:

• Business users

• Age 22–55

• Never used a xyzPhone

• Expressed interest in learning more or purchasing a xyzPhone

• Use the Web at least 10 hours a week

Draft screener

Schedule

• Recruiting starts on March 12, 2012

• Study day: March 26, 2012

• Results delivery: April 2, 2012

Script (TBD)

A short plan that you and your stakeholders prepare together is a bare minimum to a successful start of a research project. Let's discuss one important aspect of the plan: the study goal.

Study goals

A study goal is the high-level reason (or reasons) for conducting a study. Goals should be carefully crafted as a single coherent sentence. If you have two goals, try to fit them into one sentence. If you have three or four goals, create a numbered list with very short goal statements. If you have more than three or four goals, you are either aiming too high (meaning that you have too many goals) or you are repeating yourself. In the former case, try to divide your study into two or more smaller studies. In the latter, consolidate your repeated goals into one tight goal.

Here is an example of goals that repeat themselves:

- Identify pain points and delights users have with product X.

- Uncover product X's usability successes and failures.

- Develop a prioritized list of what works and what doesn't work for users with product X.

Why have goals? Who needs goals?

Goals help stakeholders understand your intentions. When in doubt about what to focus on, study goals help everyone focus. They are best used as a tool for creating a common language and setting expectations. On one hand, they are high-level enough to communicate what a study is about. On the other hand, they are not too detailed and might be perceived as vague. That's okay. They don't have to be too explicit.

Nongoals

When you think it is important to state what the study will not achieve, add a brief description of nongoals. Nongoals help everyone understand what the team is not after. For example, if the goal of a usability test is to identify what works well as well as what works not so well with a certain design, a nongoal might be understanding what the most frequently used feature is in the product. The reason, by the way, is that a usability test is not the best methodology for capturing data about product usage. Log analysis or a survey might be a better way to achieve this goal.

The difference between goals and questions

If the goal is the mission of the study, research questions specify what information study results will provide. Good research questions are one notch more detailed than study goals. Table 3.2 demonstrates the main differences between goals and questions.

Table 3.2 The main differences between goals and research questions		
	Study goals	**Research questions**
Level of detail	High level	Specific
Length	1–3 goals	3–10 questions
Function	• Help define research questions • Create common language • Set expectations	• Help define study script • Set expectations
Phrased as	Statements	Questions

The following story demonstrates what happens when questions are not defined in advance and how the researcher found a way to minimize client pushback for study results when no clear goals are set.

SETTING TESTING GOALS WITH A TEAM OR CLIENT

Kris Engdahl, Usability Manager, athenahealth, United States

As a consultant, I saw testing projects that started with the description of the project from the proposal. "Company X wants to ensure that their new website is as easy to use as possible." The kickoff meeting would go smoothly, but when we would send the client a draft of the tasks, the drafts would come back with several new tasks added, or suggestions that would take the test in a whole new direction. "Why don't we have them just free explore and see where they go?" or "Make them click this link – we should have them look at the Humpty Dumpty page, too." Similar iterations occurred with the screener.

I realized that the client was clarifying the goals of the test in their iterations of the script and the screener. I learned to always first clarify the goals. It makes the rest of the project go much more smoothly.

In the initial meeting, I probe to find out what my "clients" want to know from the test. I keep eliciting responses until the team says something like, "that's about all" or "that's what we want to know right now." I list the test goals as questions and distribute them to the team within one working day for their review. If the list is long, I ask them to prioritize the list.

When I write the test script, I tie each task to the list of goals, and I list a maximum time for each task. I send the tasks to the team, with the times totaled. If the tasks exceed the session length, I ask the team to identify tasks to trim from the test plan.

When it's time to report the results, I focus on answering the questions that we set out as the testing goals. My executive summary can sometimes be as simple as listing the initial questions and their short answers.

Since I've started setting these goals with my teams and clients, I've had quicker test preparation, and I get very little pushback from clients and internal teams in the results presentation.

Here is an example for a website test with Retirement Calculator.

Goals: This study will test the Retirement Calculator, focusing on the navigation and the effectiveness of the messaging. Specifically, we will answer the following questions:

1. Do participants notice the calculator link on the home page? Are they drawn to it?

2. Can they find the way to launch the calculator?

3. What is their initial response to the calculator?

4. Do they navigate through the calculator steps easily?

5. Do they understand how to interact with the sliders to see how to address a shortfall?

6. Are the shortfall graphs clear?

7. Do they notice and click More Options?

8. What do they want to know next?

Tasks

Task	Purpose
Intro, briefing, snacks	Standard
Pretest questionnaire	Get more info about participant
Task 1: Page exploration	Test visibility, salience of calculator
Task 2: Bring up calculator	Test findability of calculator
Task 3: Navigate through calculator	Test navigation, interaction, clarity of graphs
Task 4: Find a way to reach the goal of 100% coverage for retirement	Test use of sliders, use of "More Options," clarity of graphs
Task 5: Edit info (increase withholding)	Test findability of "Edit Info"
Posttest questions and SUS (System Usability Scale)	Overall feedback, ease of use perceptions
Total time	

Goals are short statements that help clients understand at a very high level why a research project is planned. They help everyone understand what the team is after. Now let's move to something that I consider to be the heart and soul of any study plan: the list of research questions.

Research questions

Research questions are the center of every research activity. They are the core of a study plan and the one section that needs most of your attention, as well as that of your stakeholders. They define the specifics of what you are after, they help you tighten your script, and they stop you from drifting away to irrelevant areas.

When you develop questions, start with what you learned during the kick-off meeting with your stakeholders. Remember when you asked them what they wanted to learn in this study? Their answers should help you come up with research questions. Think of the research questions as titles in your study results report. They should be specific, yet not too long. It is extremely important that your stakeholders understand that these questions are not necessarily ones you will actually ask study participants. When you have a question such as, "Do users understand the sign-up process?" you don't ask study participants this exact question. Otherwise, you put them in an uncomfortable situation if they don't understand the process. If they do understand it, they might think you are patronizing them. You will probably ask other questions to get the answers your stakeholders are looking for.

Good and bad questions

Bad research questions can put you in an uncomfortable situation. They might make people perceive you as untrustworthy or unprofessional or as someone who is not the sharpest pencil in the drawer. Surprisingly, great research questions will not work in the opposite way: they will not make you look smart, rich, young, or happy. But they will help solve important problems.

One or more of the following attributes characterizes a bad research question:

- **Not related to the study goal.** If you are anything like me, you are very curious. Yes, it would be extremely interesting to learn about all these things, but when it comes to research questions, you need to let go. Choose only questions that help your stakeholders meet the goal of the study.

    - Bad: Research questions focus on identifying user needs when the goal is to identify usability successes and failures with a certain design.

    - Good: Research questions focus on identifying what makes participants complete a certain process when goal is to identify usability successes and failures with a certain design.

- **Phrased so that the answer is either "yes" or "no."** With this type of phrasing, your stakeholders will not be interested in anything else but the short answer. Reality is more complicated than just "yes" or "no."

- Bad: Are the options on the navigation bar discoverable?

- Better: How discoverable are the navigation bar options?

The exception here is a list of research questions for products used in highly regulated environments (e.g., aerospace, healthcare, nuclear plants) that might be phrased as "yes" and "no" questions.

- **Too vague.** Remember, this is the time to be more specific.

  - Bad: What are the usability issues of the sign-up process?

  - Good:

    – What makes participants successfully complete the sign-up process?

    – What makes participants fail to complete the sign-up process?

- **Can't be measured.** This characteristic is not relevant to every study or research question. In cases in which it is relevant, it can really help make a question vivid.

  - Bad: Can participants successfully complete the sign-up process?

  - Good: What percentage of participants complete the sign-up process in less than two minutes with no more than three minor mistakes?

Great research questions are also:

- **As short and concise as possible.** It's easier for you and everyone else involved to figure them out quickly.

- **Phrased as a question.** You'd be amazed at how many research "questions" are really statements, not questions. For example, "Participants can complete the sign-up process." Other than the obvious fact that this research question is not a question, it also assumes that participants are successful, which might not be the case. This kind of phrasing might lead to unmet stakeholder expectations and – in extreme situations – to moderation biases. The latter happens when the study moderator leads participants to believe they are expected to succeed.

Although it is critical to carefully phrase and select research questions, it is also important to negotiate with your stakeholders about which questions to ask.

ASKING THE RIGHT QUESTIONS

Jen McGinn, Principal Usability Engineer, Oracle, United States

I had given a 30-minute presentation on what personas were and how they were used. The client team was excited but unsure how it would all work.

I had my own reservations, too. This was a group in which numerical and statistical data was critical to getting buy-in, and persona development is traditionally a qualitative method that often borders on creative writing. They needed data, but they needed it quickly – the marketing information that they did have was spotty and in some cases years old; as a result, there was no way to resolve conflicts between contradictory data.

The curriculum managers had done what research they could by attending customer conferences, but how could they know whether the customers they spoke to were representative of a larger audience? Or a valuable audience? They couldn't know, which is why personas seemed like such a good framework for organizing the disparate data points.

Looking at the kinds of data that personas typically contain, such as age, computer proficiency, outside interests, and so on, we could conceivably create a set of personas that would be interesting but not particularly useful to the client team. The key to making the personas useful, we thought, was to help the team reach their goals – specifically, revenue goals. To find out what we could do to help get them there, we posed these questions:

- What are the problems that you are trying to solve?

- What don't you know about your customers that you wish you did?

- What are the biggest challenges facing you in the coming year?

- What data would help you face those challenges?

The answers to these questions each became an attribute of the personas. For example, how much did they spend on training last year? Who approved their training budget? What certifications did they hold, and did they value them?

> After more than 1,300 survey responses and 30 interviews, we had our answers. Some information came in as expected, but much of it was new. The client team took the posters that we created, blew them up to 2 × 3 feet, and hung them around the conference rooms in which they presented. As a result, *the client team* became the persona advocates because they had been engaged from the very beginning and because we tied our research to their business – to what they were trying to achieve and to helping them meet those goals (McGinn & Kotamraju, 2008).

The questions stakeholders ask and the ones they do not

Research questions originate from two primary sources: your stakeholders and you. In many cases, stakeholders have excellent and relevant questions. On the other hand, sometimes (definitely not always) they don't ask the right ones or don't ask anything at all. When the latter is happening, it is your responsibility to work with your stakeholders toward the right list of questions to answer with UX studies. Things that will help you do that include:

- Listening carefully and identifying knowledge gaps.

- Asking what's most important.

- Asking what decisions are going to be made after study results are in.

- Figuring out (together) why certain questions are more important than others.

- Discussing why certain questions cannot be answered within certain time-frames (for example, due to a limited time to launch a product).

- Discussing questions that might change the way you think about a study. Maybe as you discuss these things further with your stakeholders, you will suddenly realize that you need to conduct a whole different study than what you had imagined.

- Conducting a premortem: ask, "If our study ends up with results we can't use, why would that be?"

Having a discussion with your stakeholders is a great opportunity to shape and tighten the list of research questions to be answered in a study. It is usually a perfect time to learn what's important to your stakeholders and for them to learn what's possible (and impossible) with practical research.

How many questions?

As a ballpark estimate, you should probably not have more than ten questions and preferably around five questions. Having a list of more than ten questions is probably too much, although some stakeholders would be happy to do more with one study. A long list will confuse and overwhelm you and your stakeholders. It'll be harder for everyone to understand what's important, what isn't so important, and what is the focus of the study. It is perfectly legit and reasonable to start with a list of 45 research questions. This list should serve only as a brain dump. The next logical step would be to shorten it – at least for the study you are currently planning.

When you have long lists of questions, go over them, think, and decide what's next. If most questions are not that important, try to consolidate and prune them into a tightened list. This is a great exercise that will focus the study as a whole. On the other hand, if most questions are important, it's a good time to prioritize and divide them into logical chunks. When you have a long list of important questions, you are in fact developing a research program that consists of several studies. Each study will answer a different group of questions. This way, you keep each study's list of questions short, focused, and – most important – achievable.

Prioritizing questions

When you finally have a short list of research questions or a long list that has been split into a few studies, you can do two things to prioritize them:

1. **List them in order of importance.** I know it's an obvious thing to say. I just want to emphasize why the order might become useful. One member of your study team is Murphy. He always shows up at the most critical times. Things happen, especially in studies involving humans. You might not be able to get answers to everything you planned for. When questions appear in order of importance, you know which ones you can skip when Murphy shows up.

2. **Divide them into two groups.** When you have more than seven or eight questions, consider dividing them into two priority groups. The first one is the primary group of questions. These are questions that must be answered during the study; otherwise, the goal is not met. The second group consists of secondary questions that will be answered if time permits. It's just a clearer way of prioritizing your list of questions and setting the right expectations. It'll help you as well as your stakeholders.

Now that you have fleshed out goals and research questions, it's a great time to match a methodology to help everyone get those answers.

Selecting a methodology and describing it

Now that you are perfectly aligned with your stakeholders with regard to the goals of the study and the questions it is going to answer, it is a great time to select a methodology. If your stakeholders and you have been working together for a while, this part of planning a study is probably going to be relatively smooth. If you are partnering with stakeholders new to the UX research world, you want to ease their way into the field by not attacking them with UX jargon. In many cases, you will have to negotiate the way to the most practical research methodology. Sometimes you might rightly argue that certain questions could be answered only with certain methodologies. In other cases, your stakeholders might rightly argue that they don't have time to wait or funding available for certain methodologies. This negotiation stage is a precious opportunity to share and pass knowledge in both directions. You are learning about engineering capabilities and limitations and about business priorities and opportunities. In exchange, your stakeholders learn about your toolkit of research methodologies and their advantages and drawbacks.

The following story from Germany shows how one client request can translate into three very different research methodologies.

ONE REQUEST,
THREE METHODOLOGIES

Jakob Biesterfeldt, Director of International Practice, User Interface Design, Germany

A client calls. She has worked on a new website release over the last couple of months. "We want to understand how well our users can use the new navigation concept, what they think about the visual design, and whether the content meets their needs and expectations," she says. These questions require different research methods. Here is how: if we need to understand how well users can work with the new navigation concept, we need to observe real users doing real tasks with the new navigation concept. We need a working prototype and a handful of users to observe and understand any usability pitfalls in the new concept. This is a typical usability test. As for the visual design, you are looking for opinions, so you will need more responses than those from the usability test in order to get an idea of the predominant likes and dislikes of your audience. Your goal might have been to produce a visual design that is modern, not too technical, and sophisticated. No two users have the same understanding of these words, so in addition to likes and dislikes, you will need to establish a comparable design reference. We could use focus groups or surveys and use associative techniques such as, "This design looks like [another famous brand]" or "This design would suit [famous person]." Now for content: you want to understand which content is mandatory, which is nice to have, and which is useless. Again, the variety of possible answers from all users would require us to collect answers from many users, not just some. We could use contextual interviews or focus groups to understand users' needs and expectations. Different research questions, different methods. The challenge: integrate all methods into a project plan that meets the client's schedule and budget.

Stakeholders who insist that they conduct a study by implementing a methodology that does not match the questions they asked have discouraged many researchers. I recommend that these researchers change their perception of reality. Take such a case as an opportunity for a fruitful discussion, not one for picking a fight. You want to be smart, not right. Learn from your stakeholders. Listen to them. Provide reasonable arguments for what different methodologies are good for.

The following story about a study conducted in India demonstrates how the researcher diverted the discussion from focusing on methodology first to coming up with clear research questions.

NEGOTIATING A METHODOLOGY FOR A MILK STUDY IN INDIA

Meena Kothandaraman, Adjunct Professor, Human Factors in Information Design Program, Bentley University, United States

Promethean Power Systems, a Cambridge, Massachusetts, startup, set out to identify the best way to integrate their solar-powered instantaneous cooling system into the Indian dairy industry. In some collection points across India, milk remains unchilled for hours until it reaches the dairy processing plant. The system would be used in off (electric) grid areas, enabling the instantaneous cooling of milk at these collection points.

Promethean needed to design the interface between the dairy farmers and the cooling system. How would the cooling system integrate with the Indian dairy process? Initially, the need for "some field study" was discussed. Company founders moved quickly to thinking interviews? Or perhaps focus groups? However, there was no clear definition of the users of the current system, or the current dairy collection process. The cooling system would have to work with these two components to ensure success. Some groundwork was needed in advance of identifying research methods. To address this issue, information-gathering sessions were held with company founders. Key topics included:

- Who were the users, and how could they be defined as personas? (Farmers, milk collection attendants, rickshaw drivers, milk truck drivers, mainte-nance personnel, etc.)

- What was the current process of getting milk from the source to the processing plant?

- What would be the impact on the personas and process when integrating the cooling system?

- Could studying local US dairies be useful? How would cultural sensitivities be measured?

- Was it even appropriate to compare and contrast US and Indian dairy industry processes?

Answers obtained from the data-gathering sessions led to greater clarity in the research method identification process. The sessions helped to generate questions that required further validation with real constituents in the Indian dairies.

As a result of this approach, two research methods were proposed to ensure robust data: contextual inquiry (CI) and surveys. CI sessions would offer unique perspectives into each persona's interaction with the current dairy process. Personas could then be probed for their perspective on the new process. Cultural inputs critical to the design of the cooling system would surface due to running the study with Indian dairy farmers. A survey (run like structured interviews to address low English-literacy rates) could ensure responses to standard questions that could be normalized across personas in different dairy collection models.

Using this process, Promethean was able to obtain valuable research data that gave input to their cooling system's interface.

Because the number of types of research methodologies is finite, here are sample descriptions of some of the methodologies practitioners frequently use which you can use in your research plans and when you describe them to stakeholders in your discussions. Three things to notice in these descriptions: they are short, they do not use UX jargon, and they only describe the "what" will be done, not the "why." Feel free to use them in your plans after adjusting them to your unique needs.

Usability testing. Eight 60-minute one-on-one sessions will be held with product users in a usability lab. During the sessions, study participants will be asked to perform five tasks while thinking out loud. They will then be debriefed and interviewed about their experience.

Field study (ethnography, contextual inquiry). A three-member team from our company will conduct 12 two-hour visits at users' homes. During these visits, the team will first observe how users perform task 1, task 2, and task 3. Afterward, study participants will walk the study team through different artifacts (such as systems, printouts, and spreadsheets) that they use, and finally, participants will be interviewed briefly. Following each visit, the study team will conduct a 15-minute debriefing session.

Survey. A ten-question survey will be fielded through direct email to our entire existing user base. The survey will take five minutes to complete and we expect 1 percent of our users (about 500 people) to complete it.

Interviews. A series of 16 prescheduled 30-minute interviews will be held in the upcoming ABC conference in Rome, Italy, with potential users. Interviews will mostly include open-ended questions.

Cognitive walkthrough. Three product users will participate in a one-hour session, during which a task will be presented, as well as a prototype. Participants will answer three questions: what will they do next, what do they expect to happen, and what feedback do they have. The next screen will be presented based on participant answers and the three questions will be asked again. This step will go on until the task is complete.

Diary study. A three-week diary study will be held with expert users. Participants will be asked to post from four to six diary entries describing their experience when they first use the new Groups feature. Diary entries will be posted through a private blog and will cover any relevant topic participants feel they should share.

Participatory design. A two-hour meeting will be held, during which key product stakeholders (including product managers, software developers, sales rep, marketing manager) and three product users brainstorm design solutions. The primary deliverable of the meeting is a rough sketch for the main design challenge at stake. (Note that this is just a sample participatory design activity.)

Focus group. A 90-minute group activity and discussion will take place with six potential product customers. The group moderator will introduce a topic to the group participants and direct them to work in two teams on a collage around the presented topic. Each team will then present their collage and a discussion will be held. (Note that this is just a sample focus group activity.)

Card sorting. A series of 20 thirty-minute one-on-one sessions with our existing website users will be held in our headquarters. Study participants will be given 50 cards, each with a name of a page in our website. They will be asked to sort the cards into logical groups and name each group while thinking out loud. A recommended structure for the site will be calculated and group names will be analyzed.

Eye tracking. A series of 30 sixty-minute one-on-one sessions will be held with product users in the usability lab while using an eye tracker. During the sessions, study participants will be asked to perform six tasks while their eye movements and fixations are tracked.

A/B testing (split testing or live experiments). Fifty percent of our usual website traffic will be diverted into a different design of the sign-up process. Various usage metrics will be tracked and logged.

Online study (unmoderated, using UserZoom, etc.). An email invitation to participate in an online study will go out to 10,000 website users who meet a set of predefined criteria. When participants click the study link, they will be taken to the study environment and will read instructions and answer an opening questionnaire. Half of the participants will then complete three tasks with our website; the other half will complete the same tasks with our primary competitor's website. Participants' actions and responses to task-related questions will be recorded and analyzed. The study will require a 20-minute effort, and we expect 3 percent of our users (about 300 people) to complete it.

A topic that I don't cover in this book is matching questions to a methodology. It is an extremely important topic that is out of the scope of this book. Have a look at the references list at the end of this chapter, where I've included an excellent resource for further reading about this important topic (Quesenbery 2008). One thing I would like to say is that you need to make sure you are right. In other words, make sure that *you* did your own research with regard to the methodology you are recommending for a given study.

When it comes to planning and engaging your stakeholders, there's one thing you can do that can make magic: adding a quantitative aspect to your study. You won't regret it. Let's discuss why.

The magic of injecting quantitative data into qualitative findings

When you plan to use a qualitative methodology for your research, put some time aside to think about how you can add a quantitative angle to support the qualitative findings. I realize that I sound pretty confident when I recommend this approach.

I am confident, because I have witnessed the wonders of how a little quantitative injection affects business and engineering stakeholders. Don't get me wrong. I'm not saying that all of your stakeholders are data-driven. I do know, however, that when a qualitative finding is hooked up with a relevant quantitative one, "a-ha!" moments are more likely to happen.

 Watch my interview with Meena Kothandaraman, Adjunct Professor at Bentley University and a usability consultant. Meena argues that the biggest value to stakeholders is identifying a gap that users have, quantifying it, and measuring it to show how it is closed after launching or redesigning a product. Use QR code 127 to access the video, a quick summary of the interview, and Meena's biography.

Here are a few ideas for combining quantitative data into qualitative findings:

1. When you find in a field study that people hardly use a certain aspect of your company's website, support this finding with log analysis of actual usage.

2. When your support team keeps informing you and other stakeholders that customers are dissatisfied with a product, run a survey among a representative sample of the user population to see how happy they are.

3. When you conduct a standard, traditional usability test in a lab, track and calculate participants' "lostness." A lostness score informs you how lost people are when they try to complete a task (Tullis & Albert 2008). It basically takes into account the minimum and actual number of steps to complete a task. Stakeholders love this.

4. Identify unique UX metrics and track, measure, and use them when you communicate with stakeholders. For example, number of user sighs per task completed.

5. Combine attitudes gathered in a focus group with performance data (Caplan 1990).

The following example shows how three users and the addition of a qualitative aspect to an observational study helped some stakeholders make better design decisions.

Watch my interview with Jeff Sauro, Principal at Measuring Usability. Jeff is the most knowledgeable person about the intersection between usability and statistics I know. Jeff urges researchers to quantify their outputs to make them easier for stakeholders to understand. According to Jeff, any qualitative study can benefit from a numerical aspect. Use QR code 115 to access the video, a quick summary of the interview, and Jeff's biography.

HOW THREE USERS HELPED SOLVE A PROBLEM THAT 3,000 COULD NOT

Jeff Sauro, Principal, Measuring Usability LLC, United States

Just because your methods are qualitative doesn't mean that you can't quantify the impact. Putting metrics around the results of your user research improves credibility and visibility. For example, Autodesk, maker of the popular design software AutoCAD, noticed a large spike in support calls related to a trial version of their software. A small observational study was conducted in which 11 users were watched remotely as they downloaded and installed the trial version of their popular architecture design software.

During the study, 3 of 11 users downloaded the wrong version of the software for their operating system. The result was an inscrutable error message during installation (which often leads to a call to support). A short discussion with these three users revealed that they were clicking the wrong button. It turns out that the "correct" button didn't look clickable enough. The trial download page had already been extensively tested and through several design iterations. This qualitative method revealed a major design problem – but the sample size was small, could we trust these results?

There is an erroneous impression that you can't have statistically valid results with such small samples and qualitative methods. How do we know these three users didn't just happen to be a fluke? After all, eight users did manage to find the correct button and download the right version.

Using the data from this study, we can generate a confidence interval around the number of users that would potentially also have this problem. We can be 95 percent confident that the actual number of users experiencing this problem is between 9 percent and 57 percent (Sauro 2005). In other words, we can be rather certain (and statistically confident) that *at least* 9 percent of users are also having a problem finding the right button. In fact, it is more likely that a much larger percentage of users are having the problem.

A new design was quickly created and uploaded to the site. An A/B test revealed that the new design was generating a 5 percent higher conversion rate. More users were finding the right button!

For a page with such high traffic, small differences translate into big differences in revenue. A small sample qualitative research study was able to reveal a statistically significant conclusion and solve a major design problem.

The following example discusses arguments you can use when you try to persuade stakeholders to measure the user experience.

A CONVERSATION ABOUT NUMBERS

Bill Albert, Director, Design and Usability Center, Bentley University, United States

One of the most fascinating conversations I have with clients is about whether there is a need to measure the usability or user experience of a product. This conversation typically goes in one of two directions. As a usability consultant, I begin by highlighting the importance of measurement, particularly in the context of working to achieve specific business objectives. It is unusual to reach any resistance at this point. Then, one of two different things will happen.

Sometimes the clients will nod their heads in total agreement, wondering why they didn't measure usability before because it makes perfect sense. This is the easy conversation – it just boils down to logistics, and budgets of course, but the intention is always good. Alternatively, sometimes clients will instead question the entire premise that usability is something that should or even can be measured. They believe that usability is all about improving products (which it is) but will miss the big picture. They see usability testing as simply another step in the design/development process. It is just another box on a checklist. The strongest argument I can make in these situations is to question their assumptions. I will ask them, "How do you really know your new design is better than the old design? How do you really know your new design will achieve its intended business objectives?" Without data, these questions are unanswerable. Of course, there are plenty of hunches and gut feels. But why would someone not want to spend 1 percent of their development budget on validating their new designs? Maybe I am just too logical, but it seems like a very small price to pay to sleep well at night knowing that the rest of the 99 percent of the money was well spent.

Another way to inject quantitative magic into your work is to conduct studies with the sole purpose of measuring something or looking at a certain metric. The following story is an excellent implication of this approach.

THE COST OF FINDING DOCUMENTS

Shmuel Bollen, Human Factors Analyst, Bose Corporation, United States

A number of years ago, I championed an intranet redesign. Our grassroots intranet needed some top-down structure, but there was little appetite to devote resources to the project. In order to gain support, I conducted an analysis of the current state. I first examined the logs to find the top ten most commonly used documents. I then asked 20 users to try to find those documents and calculated an average time-to-find for each one. I then multiplied that average time by the number of times each document had been accessed in the previous year. Using that number and a fringed hourly rate, I was able to calculate a "Cost of Finding" metric for the top ten documents. Because there was no intranet search engine for security reasons, navigation and bookmarking were the only options for locating documents.

This metric became my "elevator pitch." I was able to project the metric based on corporate growth plans, and it quickly became apparent to management that the project would be a worthwhile cost-reduction effort. I conducted a card-sorting exercise, then a paper prototype based on those results. The paper prototype showed a significant average reduction in "Cost to Find" per document. The project was approved, the design was deployed, and I used the metric for several years to show the ongoing benefit of the research.

REFERENCES

Caplan, S.H., 1990. Using focus group methodology for ergonomic design. Ergonomics 33, 5.

McGinn, J. & Kotamraju, N., 2008. Data-driven persona development. CHI 2008 Proceedings, ACM Conference on Human Factors in Computing Systems, Florence, Italy, April 5–10, 2008. <http://blogs.oracle.com/jen/resource/McGinn_BostonCHI_Presentation.pdf> (accessed 8/25/11).

Quesenbery, W., 2008. Choosing the right usability technique: Getting the answers you need. A workshop for User Friendly 2008 Conference, Shenzhen, China.

Sauro, J., 2005. Confidence interval calculator for a completion rate. <http://www.measuringusability.com/wald.htm> (accessed 8/26/11).

Tullis, T., Albert, B., 2008. Measuring the user experience: Collecting, analyzing, and presenting usability metrics. Morgan Kaufman, Burlington, MA.

TAKEAWAYS

In this chapter, I discussed planning studies with stakeholders through a short, written document that includes goals, research questions, and the chosen methodology. Here are the main points:

1. A research plan provides a blueprint for the planned research activity.

2. Working with stakeholders on a study plan is a great opportunity to learn from and with them about the need for a study.

3. Sharing a study plan with stakeholders should happen early and often.

4. Long plans are not necessarily bad. If you write a long plan, make sure you have a very good reason for it.

5. When you decide not to write a study plan, make sure it's for the right reason – for example, because the team is already aligned with you, not because you wish to avoid debate or save time.

6. Write a one-page plan with the following sections:
   - Title, author, and date
   - Background
   - Goals
   - Research questions
   - Methodology
   - Schedule
   - Script placeholder

7. Good research questions are more detailed than study goals.

8. Research questions are the heart and soul of the study plan. Phrase them carefully. Have no more than ten questions.

9. Describe the study methodology very briefly, without using UX jargon, and include only the "what" (will be done), not the "why."

10. Try to create an opportunity to support qualitative research with quantitative measurements and numbers. It'll add strength to the study findings.

CHAPTER 4

What's gonna work?
Teamwork!

**HANDS-ON TECHNIQUES FOR COLLABORATING AND
INVOLVING STAKEHOLDERS IN RESEARCH PLANNING,
EXECUTION, ANALYSIS, AND REPORTING**

twitter **Anonymous**

thinks UXers, including myself, believe
we are far more open to collaboration
than we really are.

Introduction

Many people look for sound bites or punch lines, for the winning argument they can use with stakeholders that will fully persuade them to act upon research findings or to even invest in research at all. The UX community is known for sharing knowledge and experience in many different ways and channels. Once in a while, you read about really good arguments you can use in your next stakeholder meeting. I don't like that approach. I don't think you can persuade people by using one-liners. It's just trying to show them (and yourself maybe) you are smarter than them and that you argue well. I believe in legwork, hard work, and profound collaboration. When you work *with* stakeholders, not *on* them, everyone stands to gain.

The best time to collaborate with stakeholders depends on how successful you want to be. Figure 4.1 reflects my personal experience. A green cell means that you collaborate with stakeholders in a certain research stage; red means you don't. So, for example, if you want everybody to win (i.e., research is fully integrated and accepted by the organization), you should collaborate in all stages of research, from planning to reporting and follow-up. On the other hand, if you are not collaborating with stakeholders in all of these stages, you will fail. Yes, there are gray areas. If you only collaborate during planning, reporting, and follow-up, the level of uptake and consumption of UX research will not be ideal, but at the same time, it will not be too bad. This chart helps evaluate your organization's UX research uptake health. Try using it yourself. How much do you collaborate? What is the resulting success level? Are you happy with it? Should you collaborate more?

	Planning	Recruiting	Execution	Analysis	Reporting	Follow-up
FAIL						
Lame						
Meh						
Yay						
WIN						

Figure 4.1: When is the best time to collaborate? The chart crosses research stages with buy-in success from FAIL to WIN based on research collaboration with stakeholders. A green cell means that you collaborate with your stakeholders in this stage; red means you don't.

 Watch my interview with Bertice Berry, a sociologist, author, lecturer, and educator from Atlanta. Bertice says we sometimes make research The Thing. Nobody connects with it. The point of connection is between two people – not between people and research. Use QR code 136 to access the video, a quick summary of the interview, and Bertice's biography.

This chapter will guide you through ideas and techniques for collaborating more with UX research stakeholders from planning through participant recruiting and joint data collection, all the way to analyzing study results and reporting them together to other stakeholders.

Why collaborate?

Many researchers understand that planning studies with their stakeholders and clients is highly beneficial for many reasons. They know that the more they share, listen, accept, and learn from stakeholders during the early stages of a research project, the higher the chances that stakeholders will act upon study findings when these become available. In my experience, collaborated planning can get you only that far. Researchers plan a study with their stakeholders, then desert them and run the study by themselves, only to come back to stakeholders a month later expecting them to fix usability problems, change the product roadmaps, or stop a release of a major redesign. I'm sorry to break the harsh news. It doesn't work this way. Yes, your stakeholders might have had the best intentions and they truly, profoundly cooperated, and signed off on a study plan. But things change. C'est la vie. Priorities change in a second. It only takes a second to make a U-turn. And when you come back with your results a month later, you probably find that nobody is waiting for you. They moved on, made their design decisions, and coded them (or built the thing if the product is not digital). Even if it takes you a week to complete a study, not a month, it will still be the same.

 Watch my interview with Takashi Sasaki, Partner at Infield Design, Japan. Takashi-san remembers that shortly after Infield Design was founded, they used to get a design brief from clients on day 1 of a project. They then went on and conducted research, which they presented with great excitement. They were puzzled when clients didn't understand what they were talking about. They then realized it is hard to translate research results from one person to another without profound collaboration. Use QR code 121 to access the video, a quick summary of the interview, and Takashi's biography.

If stakeholders are *not* involved in the following activities, then they are not going to be fully committed to acting upon the study recommendations:

- Determining who participates in the study

- Interacting with study participants

- Co-analyzing the data collected

- Reporting results to others with you

Let's look at it in terms of risk. The more you involve stakeholders in research, the less risk you are taking that they will not act upon research results. And vice versa: the less you involve them, the more risk you are taking.

Next, I discuss different opportunities for collaborating with stakeholders. These will increase their commitment to act upon findings and also enrich you as a professional, improve your work environment and relationships, and sometimes win you friends and help you influence people.

Plan together

Collaborating with stakeholders when research plans are formed is a great opportunity to identify the right research needs and tailor relevant plans to support your team's efforts with UX studies. To engage your stakeholders with research planning, you need to attend and initiate ongoing meetings, be creative in using collaboration methodologies, and develop collaboration artifacts.

The meetings you need to have

There are several meetings you should have on a regular basis. These are meetings that will help you better understand the team you belong to and help you and your stakeholders create relevant research plans together. They also serve another important purpose: they help other team members get to know you. It's so much easier to collaborate with a familiar face.

Meetings you initiate

These are meetings you must have with specific stakeholders. Usually, these are one-on-one or one-on-two meetings that (in most cases) should not take longer than 30 minutes:

1. **High-level research planning** with a senior product or engineering manager. The purpose of this meeting is to gather strategic insights into the business and technology of the product/company. I suggest that you make sure the senior stakeholders you meet have a full understanding of what you are trying to get out of the meeting in advance. By the end of the meeting, you should have a clear idea of direction and priorities for your research plans. Or at least you will know whom to talk with to get them. This meeting should happen once a month or a quarter.

2. **Tactical research planning and updates** with a product manager or engineering team lead. This meeting goes one level down from the previous high-level meeting. The goal here is to make sure that on the tactical level, key stakeholders know what you do, why, and when. By the end of this meeting, you might have answers to burning day-to-day research-related questions such as, "How can we find more study participants?" or "What are the most important parts of the product that require lab evaluation?" This meeting should happen once every week or two.

Meetings you attend

These are meetings you attend but at which you usually aren't an active partici-pant. Attend these meetings to better understand what is going on in the team, the dynamics between stakeholders, what's currently bothering people, and why. The valuable information you gather in such meetings can help you better support your team's effort with research studies:

1. **Weekly product management meeting** with product managers and their manager (Director or VP level, depends on the size of the company).

2. **Weekly engineering leadership meeting** with engineering team leads and their manager (director or VP level). This is an interesting meeting for you as a UX practitioner. You will probably not understand 90 percent of what's being said because engineers usually speak the language of technology. Many UXers roll their eyes to the sky when they have to attend a technical meeting. Take it as an opportunity to learn about technology and about what's important to engineer-ing leaders. The more you attend these meetings, the better you are able to understand technology. In time, you will gain credibility when you start speak-ing your stakeholders' language.

What not to do?

One thing you should avoid is thinking that it's enough to attend company-wide meetings in which strategic directions are presented. Yes, you will learn about these directions, but usually by the time they are presented, it's too late to change them. If you think big, you want to help set company strategy with research-based decision making. So don't sit back and relax thinking that you know everything you need to know. Get out of your chair and start listening to and talking with people.

A simple planning artifact

Assuming that people actually want research to happen, and that you know how to make the research fit properly into product development schedules, I recommend that once a quarter you devote about a week for planning studies for the next quar-ter. Meet people, ask questions, listen, think, and then create a draft research plan for the upcoming quarter. Share this plan with key stakeholders, collect their feed-back, and then publish the plan. This plan will change during the quarter. Don't

July	
1st-3rd	Quarterly planning
6th-10th	Study 1 prep
13th-17th	Study 1 data collection
20th-24th	Study 1 analysis
26th-30th	Study 2 prep	Study 2 data collection

August		
3rd-7th	Study 2 analysis	Study 3 prep
10th-14th	Study 3 prep	Study 3 data collection
17th-21st	Study 3 data collection	
24th-28th	Study 3 analysis	

September	
1st-4th	Study 4 prep
7th-11th	Study 4 data collection
14th-18th	Study 4 data collection
21st-25th	Study 4 analysis
28th-30th	Study 4 analysis

Figure 4.2: Quarterly UX research planning artifact.

make a fuss about it because every plan eventually changes. The key is having a plan to change from. To communicate the quarterly plan throughout the process described here, use the simple artifact demonstrated in Figure 4.2.

Notice the following aspects of this planning artifact:

1. Activity resolution is half a week. Daily planning is too silly to commit to that far in advance. A weekly or biweekly resolution might not well represent what you are doing.

2. Activities included are preparation, data collection, and analysis (which includes deliverable preparation).

3. Data collection, or user face time, is highlighted with a different background color. That's what many stakeholders are interested in. It helps them know when users are around so that they can come and observe.

I use this artifact when I communicate with stakeholders about quarterly plans. Sometimes I print it out and hand it to them, especially when it changes.

Agreement and buy-in per study

All these planning meetings and artifacts should not prevent you from making sure that you still get ad hoc agreement and buy-in per study. The fact that you planned an eye-tracking study with the director of product management doesn't mean that product managers will agree to change engineering priorities or fix certain designs following your study. You need to go through the process described in Chapter 2 (interview your stakeholders prior to planning a study to better understand the product at stake, its users, the study goals, the expected schedule, and expected actions following the study results). You already have a master plan – that's your quarterly research plan – and before each study you just make sure everybody is on board with it. You cannot expect every stakeholder to be well versed on the quarterly research plan. They have other burning priorities. It's your job to provide appropriate reminders.

After planning is done – and sometimes even shortly prior to that – you need to start recruiting participants for the study. Recruiting is a tough task, but there are people in your company who can be extremely helpful with participant recruiting.

Recruit participants together

Your goal for recruiting together is to make sure you are recruiting the right participants in the most efficient way. You want to prevent a situation in which your stakeholders claim that the results of the study are not valid or reliable because these were the wrong participants. I'm being very gentle here. I have witnessed situations in which participants were called (not to their faces) "stupid," "bad," and "dumb." When this happens, it means you have failed at getting buy-in for the study. Only if you work with your stakeholders are you able to get the right participants and the buy-in you need. Assuming that you've already set the participant characteristics with your stakeholders, let's discuss how you can get help.

Who can help and when

Recruiting the right participants for a user experience study is a challenging task. The task becomes even more challenging when there is a need to recruit users from special groups rather than the general population. For example, it is easier to recruit people who use email than people who use accounting software or an EKG machine. Even with special populations, there are various levels of recruiting challenges. The recruiting task is usually harder when the specialized user has an account manager assigned by your company. For example, it's easier to recruit users of project management software (such as MS Project) compared to recruiting users of a customer relationship management (CRM) product (such as those of Salesforce.com).

My point is that the more challenging the recruiting, the more you will need other people's help. I do not intend for this book to specify the ins and outs of recruiting. Read Nielsen's comprehensive report about recruiting study participants (2003).

When it comes to recruiting specialized users who have an account manager from your company, people in three primary functions can help you: account managers (salespeople), technical support or services people, and product managers. All of them meet and talk with the users you are looking for on a regular basis.

Asking for account managers' help is something you should do with extra care because some of them might be sensitive to a situation where someone else approaches "their" clients with different requests. Appendix A (use QR code 142 to access it) includes two practical tools for connecting and communicating with people who can help you recruit study participants.

Why bother? I can do without them!

When the company's clients have account managers (or salespeople) assigned, you might get the feeling that salespeople are protective of the entire communication with customers. What seems protective to you is not at all protective. When Sales insist you need to go through them to contact a customer, there is a very good reason for that. Customers can be difficult to handle, especially those who pay your company a lot of money. These relationships might get extremely delicate; sometimes one word said in a tone that is perceived in the wrong way might jeopardize million-dollar deals and long-term relationships. Salespeople are aware of this. You might not be. When they want to control the communication with customers, they want to make sure that customers understand who is asking what, for what reason, and how this might affect the relationship. Let salespeople do what they're best at. So when they tell you not to talk to customers, or that they will recruit for you, or that you only need to tell them what you want – you need to take a leap of faith and trust them. It might not work smoothly at first, but it will in time. When you and salespeople learn to know and trust one another, things will get a lot better, and recruiting study participants might not be such a tough task.

How to ask for help

When you meet someone who can help you recruit study participants, it's always best to meet him or her in person, if possible. Having that face-to-face aspect always improves communication. When you meet in person, you can tell very quickly whether the person you talk with is going to assist you. It's very similar to the difference between conducting research face to face compared to running remote studies.

I always start my recruiting discussions with sales managers by asking them if they are interested in having me share recent research findings with their teams. I offer a couple of recent studies that I assume will be helpful for salespeople in their client meetings – for example, if I found that the product is working extremely well for our users in a certain aspect or if I gathered data that compares our product to the competition. Generally speaking, studies that evaluate designs are usually not interesting for salespeople. Because I realize salespeople should spend their time selling, I offer to share study results in the already scheduled team meetings. I also commit to presenting for no more than ten minutes plus an additional five minutes for Q&A.

Only when I learn how I can help salespeople by giving them ammunition for their sales pitch do I turn to asking how they can assist my efforts to improve the usability and usefulness of our products. I ask for recruiting support while specifying the audiences I am interested in. Salespeople have tons of experience with clients, so I ask them for their opinion about the audience I'm looking for in the study at hand. I always hear interesting views.

What I have found to work extremely well with sales teams is the following: meet with the sales manager and discuss his or her needs as well as yours. Then, ask him or her to walk with you to where the sales team is located in the office. Some sales managers will be perfectly okay with that. Walk around with the manager, introduce yourself to salespeople, and quickly explain what you are looking for, and they will immediately respond with potential participants. That's good enough for you at this point. You'll follow up with them later on for the details.

Salespeople are very busy people

Salespeople should sell stuff and make customers happy. They are the company's front line of success. Their success creates the company's success. Think about it: salespeople have pretty much the same goal as you do. You also want to make people happy with useful, usable, and beautiful products. Time not spent selling the company's products is perceived as lost time in the eyes of sales leaders, and rightly so. On the other hand, if you are not able to recruit participants for a study, product development teams cannot benefit from user insights and cannot create those useful, usable, and beautiful products. The middle road for mutual success is mutual respect for each another's discipline. I'm not going to discuss how salespeople should behave because you cannot control that. But you can control your own behavior. Here are a few things that will demonstrate to salespeople that you are respectful of their time:

- Schedule short meetings with sales leaders once a quarter. You don't need more than 30 minutes to discuss your study plans and recruiting needs.

- Educate yourself about sales department structure and roles. Not all the people in the sales team do the same thing. Knowing who reports to whom and the different roles and responsibilities of salespeople will make a huge difference when you communicate with them.

- Join their already scheduled meetings. If you need to talk to a large group of salespeople, don't schedule a separate meeting. Instead, join a team meeting they already have and ask to grab ten minutes.

- Be a useful resource. When you communicate with salespeople, don't waste time on issues that are not supposed to interest them, just because you might think it is interesting. Put some thought into what they care about and talk about that. You will be highly appreciated for this approach.

When recruiting is done, it is time to go to the field or the lab and get all that data you are looking for. To me, interacting with study participants is the best part of my job. Why not share it with others? Especially if it helps persuade them to act upon what you find together. The next section discusses ways to involve stakeholders in field and lab studies.

Interact with users together

Stakeholders must have face time with study participants. Observing studies is the bare minimum to get their buy-in for research. I'd like to point out a few aspects of observation that you must be aware of – how many sessions you ask observers to attend, asking observers to take notes, and making it easier for them to observe.

When it comes to the actual study sessions, I almost always prefer to have stakeholders interact with study participants with me. I know some researchers think this is not a good idea. I even have some horror stories of my own. In several cases, stakeholders started arguing with participants about why they could not complete a task. In some cases, body language of stakeholders was telling participants what they should do next to complete a task. That's all true, and these valid examples should prevent you from inviting stakeholders to the study room. But I say nay. Bring them in! You want your stakeholders to have firsthand experience of the user experience, not a remote one. Here are things I do whenever I can:

- **I invite stakeholders to join me to field studies.** Despite realizing that three people are the maximum recommended number to attend a field visit (researcher and two observers), I always try to have more people join me if possible. I usually go with four additional stakeholders. I make the necessary arrangements and provide the much-needed instructions (to participants and observers) to make sure that it works well. I can't remember a time it didn't.

- **I invite stakeholders to join me in the study room,** especially if it's a remote study or a phone interview. I make sure that they are properly informed about dos and don'ts and I arrange the seating area so that participants don't have eye contact with observers. I also make sure to set the right expectations about when it is appropriate for observers to get involved in the session.

- **I encourage stakeholders to initiate meetings with users** on their own. I know some of my colleagues roll their eyes when they hear about yet another product manager who came back from a client meeting with some ideas. I'm all for it. It's great that they do that. In many cases, they find what I find or complement what I find in the studies I conduct.

- **I offer stakeholders help with phrasing their questions or surveys.** They will meet users and run surveys whether I like it or not. All I do is support them by suggesting even better ways to do just that.

The following sections provide more details about each one of these approaches.

Stakeholders in field studies

I consider it a personal failure if I go on a field study session by myself. It seems to me to be a complete waste of time. What's the point? I always have company, be it a product manager, engineers, designers, other researchers, salespeople, technical writers, support people – you name it. If they want to join, I let them. If they don't, I make them feel like they are missing an invaluable experience. I might even reschedule sessions to accommodate stakeholders' availability.

 Watch my interview with Paul Adams, a product manager at Facebook and former UX researcher. Paul claims that it is hard to engage people in field research because it is unlikely that they will join field observations conducted outside of the office. He suggests conducting dual-purpose studies in the lab. Use QR code 112 to access the video, a quick summary of the interview, and Paul's biography.

It is a norm in our field to say that no more than three people should go on a field visit: a researcher and two stakeholders. The primary reason is to not make the participant feel overwhelmed with too much of an "audience" observing them. But what if they are perfectly fine with it? What if observers are well behaved? I say it's definitely possible and even recommended having five people attend a field visit. Sometimes the office space is way too small to host even two people, and the study must be done in a meeting room or a bigger room. This is a great opportunity to bring more stakeholders to the field. Yes, my first priority is the comfort of study participants. If they feel uncomfortable, I am the first to notice and take care of it – even at the expense of a stakeholder. But my number two priority (very close to being number one) is my stakeholders. After all, if they are not engaged, nothing will come out of the study. So I do my best to have it both ways. I have never had an issue with it. It all depends on setting the right expectations with participants, their managers, and stakeholders.

The following story, from Israel, talks about something that has probably happened to anyone who has ever invited a salesperson to join a field visit – dealing with salespeople who try to defend the product when the user is providing feedback about its drawbacks.

DEALING WITH DEFENSIVE SALESPEOPLE

Yoram Pomer, Usability Expert, Israel

I work for a global company with customers all over the world. Recently, I led a research activity we call a "Usability Trip." The trip is a day-long meeting with a customer, coordinated by account managers from our company, who also join us. The goal is to discover what our users need to accomplish in their daily work. For us – the usability people – it is an opportunity to uncover user needs regardless of the current offering of our organization. All of the meetings have the same structure: first, the customer representatives introduce themselves, their background, and their role in the organization. The rest of the meeting is influenced by the tasks users perform in their daily jobs.

One of the first issues we had to deal with during the meetings was that account managers had the urge to "defend" the application each time users provided negative comments about it. Whenever users said they don't under-stand how to use a specific feature, the account manager would immediately interrupt and explain the importance of the feature and how they should use it. Each time users described a way they used the application that was differ-ent from what we originally intended, account managers corrected them.

The first time we realized there was an issue was during one of our first customer meetings. We didn't have any other choice but to interrupt the account manager's explanation and urge him to continue the explanation after the meeting ended because we still had a lot to cover. We offered both the account manager and the customer a chance to schedule a follow-up meeting. During our first break, we apologized to the account manager for interrupting him earlier and explained why it was so vital for us to hear the customer's perspective about using the system.

Our primary takeaway was that any nonusability person who joins a customer meeting must go through a short briefing to set expectations and priorities. Prior to the following meetings, we made sure that account managers understood the nature of these meetings.

One special case is a field study in a foreign country. When this is the case, and if the company you work for has the budget for it, invite even more stakeholders. As soon as they accept your invitation, they become a part of the study team. Delegate responsibility areas and get their commitment to become fully engaged in this research project. It gives me great pleasure and pride to see how people get involved and engaged in these situations. These stakeholders immediately become champions and ambassadors of UX research. I remember one engineer, shortly before we departed for an international field study, telling me that he never realized that research is such hard work. I consider these as defining moments in my career. Seriously.

Developing empathy for stakeholders is important for establishing and strengthening trust. The following story highlights a minidrama that created that bond between researchers and a stakeholder.

STAKEHOLDERS IN THE FIELD

Steve Portigal, Principal, and Julie Norvaisas, Consultant, Portigal Consulting, United States

Although the benefits of having stakeholders join us in fieldwork – seeing customers firsthand, hearing their answers, asking their own questions, developing empathy, and so on – are already well articulated elsewhere, there's a powerful second-order benefit from the experience of being in the field. In these experiences, we are with our stakeholders in unique and unpredictable circumstances. The comfort zone is left far behind once we take that important step out of the office. Even small moments of fieldwork can trigger discomfort. There's an exhilarating feeling the second before we ring a participant's doorbell. What's behind that door? Opening ourselves and our stakeholders up to the potential rewards of uncertainty opens the door, literally and figuratively, to discovery. Whether we're navigating through new neighborhoods (inevitably, despite the ubiquity of GPS technology, with varying levels of success), or sampling cuisines from dreadful to exciting, we're also discovering more about each other. During recent fieldwork in southern California, a client revealed himself to be a serious foodie and terrific restaurant bloodhound. We had a number of great customer interviews and an equal number of fantastic meals, and we learned about his professional background as well as his enthusiasm and disdain for parts of his organization – valuable insight as our working relationship progressed. But on the afternoon of his last day, the adventure took its toll. After a long day with too much time in traffic, as we circled for parking in a slightly sketchy area, all the while trying to figure out exactly where our destination was (eventually we found it – a business without any signage), he understandably lost his cool. He became red-faced and floored the accelerator, driving for several blocks until the buildings, signs, and pedestrians appeared less threatening. No harm was done and the fact that he shared his loss of control was obviously a terrific trust/bonding moment. The incident also served as a reminder of our overarching goal – we were deliberately trying to get out of our comfort zone and trying to understand our customers in provocative and surprising new ways. That we had this contained microdrama and experience of being notably uncomfortable was emblematic of the whole endeavor – not literally a data-gathering moment, but an experiential aspect of the process of seeking new truths.

I am always amazed to find out that many people who write code have never met a person who is using their code. When I realize that's the case, I suggest doing something about it. Basically, it means getting people up from their chairs and monitors and creating an opportunity for them to observe and interact with real users. When budget and time are scarce, I call these "virtual visits." A virtual visit is my humorous name for a phone interview. I call a user, put the call on the speakerphone, ask a bunch of stakeholders to join me, ask the user a series of questions, and end up letting stakeholders ask their own questions. I repeat the same questions in every "visit" and publish short reports to the entire team (use QR code 142 to access Appendix B to see the kind of questions I ask). Once in a while (usually once a quarter), I look at these summaries to see whether some trends are repeating and whether it's worthwhile pitching a product change. Even if nothing comes out of these visits (which rarely happens), they are precious merely because they make people realize that users are real. The questions, by the way, are basically there to better know the user, his or her environment, and company (if relevant), as well as to understand current pain points, delights, and wish list items: basic, yet extremely effective and informative. Another way to achieve these things is to hold in-person visits once in a while. I adopted an idea called "Field Fridays" from a colleague. Once every week (or two, or three), a group of software engineers and I go on a 90-minute visit to a customer office. The goal is to learn by observation and contextual interview, as well as answering customers' questions. It is extremely beneficial to both participants and stakeholders, and this whole initiative is always highly appreciated by higher-ups on my team. That's a classic win-win situation. I highly encourage you to try it yourself.

One thing I learned about my work is that it is extremely important to share the knowledge with team members and stakeholders who have not yet had a chance to join a virtual or in-person visit. For that, I open an internal blog where I make posts that summarize these visits. This way, other team members learn about what happened and have a chance to ask follow-up questions. It also raises interest in joining future visits. Following is an interesting example of a comment one software engineer added to a blog post for after a Field Friday visit:

> The one thing that really stood out for me was how embarrassed I was to see how bad our product was and how awkward it was for me not to be able to give good answers to any of the client's good questions.

Stakeholders in lab studies

I almost always invite stakeholders to join me in the study room. The only exception is when I expect too many of them to show up (more than three or four people). When this happens, I ask them to watch from the observation room. When I do invite them to join me, it is usually for remote study sessions or phone interviews. I make sure they are properly informed about dos and don'ts. So they know it's not appropriate to comment on participant behavior, giggle, or even use certain body language. I try to make them aware of things that bias study participants or make them feel uncomfortable.

Watch my interview with Rolf Molich, owner and manager of DialogDesign, Denmark. According to Rolf, the most engaging way to get stakeholders' attention is to have them observe a usability test, then share their observations. It is a great way to establish ownership by stakeholders. Use QR code 125 to access the video, a quick summary of the interview, and Rolf's biography.

Additional aspects of inviting stakeholders to attend a lab study:

1. **How many sessions to observe.** If I were to decide whether stakeholders are to observe either one session (out of five, six, eight, or as many as you have in a study) or none of the sessions, I'd vote for none. The reason is that observing one session completely distorts one's perception of what happened in a study. When asked by stakeholders about which session they should observe, I always say "as many as possible." I suggest they observe at least two sessions. I know that every user is unique and that stakeholders will get a much better picture when they observe more than one session. I admire stakeholders who are deeply involved in a product and choose to observe most or all of the sessions. To me, these people demonstrate true dedication to their job; they are the ones who "get" UX and how much it can positively support their efforts.

The following story shows how effective it is to have senior stakeholders observe several usability study sessions and how it can win them over.

THE POWER OF OBSERVING REAL CUSTOMERS

Gregg Almquist, Principal, eXperient Interactive & Design LLC, United States

My company was hired to assist a company redesign their consumer website because membership conversion had dropped over the last year even though traffic had increased. The company believed that the sign-up process was the culprit.

Our evaluation of the site found some issues with the sign-up process, but there were other problems. The real value of this site was its content, and we believed that it needed to be rewritten, augmented, and reorganized to help move users into the conversion tunnel. The president of the company was somewhat skeptical of our evaluation because we weren't domain experts in this field. He and his team believed that the content they provided met their users' needs. Fortunately, our case was persuasive enough that he listened to our suggested next steps.

We recommended running eight one-on-one sessions where we interviewed representative users for twenty minutes about their current situation and understanding and their needs in this area. Then we would run a typical usability test asking users to complete various tasks using a prototype of a redesigned site. We got the go-ahead and created a prototype for the new information structure. However, we used existing content from the site.

Originally, the president did not plan to attend the sessions, but at the last moment he changed his mind and came to the lab. Early sessions clearly revealed that users were struggling to understand how they could benefit from becoming a member. The benefits of membership that the company thought were compelling selling points didn't resonate with the users, and users needed more supporting content to help them decide whether to join.

After the fourth session ended, the president said that he didn't need to see any more. Watching the first four sessions felt like being "hit on the head with a hammer." (Those were his words!) He got it. For the remaining sessions, we quickly rewrote some of the primary content and made some modifications to the prototype. We gathered reaction to the changes and refined it after each session. We came away with some clear understandings about how to move forward with the redesign.

At the end of the day, the president of the company thanked us for advocating for the study. He said he was glad that he watched the sessions in person because the presentation of findings wouldn't have had the same impact.

2. **Ask observers to take notes.** Engagement means that observers are active rather than passive, even when they "just" observe. I don't know anything about your note-taking skills, but I can always use some help. Ask observers to take notes, ask them to send you an email with three things they learned after

observing a study session, ask them what surprised them. You get the point. To buy into study results, stakeholders must be a part of capturing what went on during the study.

3. **Make it easy for people to observe.** You do not need to provide excuses for people not to observe. Make it a pleasant experience. To me, observers are as important as study participants. Try and have a really nice observation room in the usability lab, have great snacks, use technology that allows you to broadcast sessions to stakeholders' desktops. Things like that help stakeholders observe the study sessions. Develop more of these that are relevant for your work environment.

 Watch my interview with Dana Chisnell, an independent researcher and consultant at UsabilityWorks. Dana claims that reports objectify users and that observing them really helps getting to stakeholder "a-ha!" moments. Use QR code 119 to access the video, a quick summary of the interview, and Dana's biography.

4. **Introductions that bias.** I ask stakeholders to not introduce themselves by role or job title to study participants. My experience is that participants respond to that in a way that makes me not trust their opinion and behavior. I have seen participants behave differently when they know that the chief product manager, "the person who started this whole product line," is in the room with them observing how they use it. It's best to just say, "Hi, my name is Joe." If participants ask about roles, just say something like, "These are all team members who are eager to learn from you about what's working well and not so well with the product."

5. **Room arrangement.** If the study is an attended one (that is, the participant is physically in the study room), I arrange the seating area so that participants don't have eye contact with observers. This way, body language (of stakeholders) is less of a challenge to handle. Figure 4.3 demonstrates an unattended session that many stakeholders observe.

6. **IM (instant messaging) questions.** When stakeholders observe a study session either remotely or in the observation room, I always ask them to IM me any

Figure 4.3: Stakeholders observe a remote usability test by Bolt | Peters (printed with permission).

question during the session. I usually take notes on a laptop so that my IM tool is open for business. That's a great way to clarify things for stakeholders, get their attention, and make them feel like an integral part of the study team.

7. **Meet the participant.** When I think it is appropriate, I invite the participants to the observation room immediately after the session is over. There, they meet the stakeholders and have a chance to answer more questions. I have found this introduction to be extremely useful because participants sometimes think that they are not being watched and thus they tend to be more open with their answers. Sometimes it is not appropriate to do so – primarily because I have a hunch that the participant needs to go home and not interact with a bunch of people about their experience. In any case, I let stakeholders know that I might do that so they are not surprised.

 Watch the video contributed by the UX team at Rabobank Group, Netherlands. The video shows a usability test in which multidisciplinary stakeholders are an integral part of the study team. Use QR code 138 to access the video, a quick summary of its content, and information about Rabobank Group.

The following example demonstrates an effective way of documenting stakeholder observations during studies that helps establish and maintain trust between team members.

THE INTERACTIVE ISSUES MATRIX: RECORDING AND ORGANIZING STAKEHOLDER OBSERVATIONS

Kirsten Robinson, User Experience Architech/Lead, Endeca Technologies, United States

When I conduct usability tests – either remotely or in a lab – I invite stakeholders to observe and take notes. We debrief after each session and I type the notes into a spreadsheet that I call the Interactive Issues Matrix. Each observer reads his or her notes aloud and I type them using a projector or online meeting software so that everyone can see. I rephrase for clarity, with the group's approval. Sometimes the group argues about what they saw, but majority rule quickly wins out.

Later, I color-code the rows by participant and add two new columns (see Table 4.1). *Category* is a specific task, widget, page, or screen. *Type* includes issue, positive finding, comment by the participant, or other information. I can then sort the spreadsheet by category and look for issues. A rainbow of colors in a category indicates frequent problems.

Table 4.1 A rainbow of issues with captcha (a challenge-response test used to ensure that a response is generated by a human rather than a computer).

Participant	Task	Observation	Category	Type
1	4	She mentions that captcha is hard to read, but understands why it's used.	Captcha	Comment
1	4	Second try: submits without entering captcha. On the third try, she is successful.	Captcha	Issue
3	4	Has problems reading the captcha – takes three tries to submit successfully due to getting the captcha wrong.	Captcha	Issue
3	4	Says he understands why captcha is needed but he hates it.	Captcha	Comment
4	4	Fills in the form; hits submit without entering the captcha.	Captcha	Issue
4	4	Notices the captcha and types it correctly, successful in submitting the form on the second try.	Captcha	Issue
5	4	On second try, she got the captcha wrong. Submitted form on third try.	Captcha	Issue

> I share the spreadsheet as an informal record of the test findings or use it as input for a report.
>
> This method is quick and collaborative and builds trust with stakeholders because they know you've captured their observations accurately.

Sometimes stakeholders want to (or have to) moderate lab studies. It can happen for different reasons. They might not have a budget to hire a researcher, or the in-house researcher might not be available. With little training, these stakeholders can get better at planning, moderating, and analyzing quick usability tests. Use QR code 140 to watch Eric Ries, the father of the Lean Startup movement, talk about how his startup ran usability tests. He talks about it so naturally, and he was the company's CTO at the time! It's so obvious to him that this is what they had to do. To get a better perspective on roles and responsibilities of UX researchers and their teams, I also recommend that you read the controversial article "Surviving Our Success: Three Radical Recommendations" (Spool 2007). Jared's second radical recommendation to UX people is to stop conducting evaluations such as basic usability testing. Instead, he claims, engineers and product managers should run them so that it becomes a part of the organization's culture. It is just something everybody knows how to do.

Sometimes stakeholders conduct their own research and meet users outside of the lab. Like it or not, this is what they do. Sometimes they are even directed to do so on an ongoing basis. The next section discusses your role in this.

Help stakeholders interview users and launch surveys

I am perfectly fine with stakeholders conducting their own interviews with users, with or without my attendance – not that anyone needs my approval for this. I am aware that some of my colleagues are not comfortable when product managers talk with users. They think that product managers are asking the wrong questions and that in many cases they ask leading questions that result in proving their own pre-interview opinions.

Watch my interview with Jared Spool, CEO and Founding Principal at UIE (User Interface Engineering). Jared argues that stakeholders should moderate usability studies, even if they do a poor job. According to Jared, poor moderating is a training problem that can easily be solved. Use QR code 116 to access the video, a quick summary of the interview, and Jared's biography.

I'm a big supporter of user interviews conducted by stakeholders. It's great that they do that. In many cases, they find what I find or complement what I find in studies I conduct. I can't understand why people fight it. I offer my help to stakeholders. I ask if they would find it useful if I reviewed the list of questions they are planning to ask. I suggest asking more questions, I suggest asking the same questions with different angles or phrasing, and so on.

As I see it, the best help I can give stakeholders for interviewing users is exposing them to the behavior versus opinion issue. I give them the don't-ask-about-future-opinions-ask-about-specific-past-and-current-behavior spiel. I say something like this:

> When you interact with a user, I have one important suggestion. Instead of asking about their opinions about something, ask about specific behavior. Or even better, observe behavior. The thing with opinion is that we as humans are kind of weak at predicting the future. When you ask a user, "Will you need feature X?" they'll give you an honest answer. The problem is that you and they have no idea if this answer is true or not. Instead, I always prefer asking, "In the past three months, did you ever want to do X but couldn't?" Then I ask them to elaborate. This way I get an answer that is based on facts that actually happened, rather than opinions that try to predict the future. I must tell you that I am not perfect at this. Sometimes I slip and ask a question in the wrong way, but then I catch myself and try to ask it in a different way. Think about it the next time you interact with a user.

Some of my UX research colleagues are not supportive of this approach. They claim that humans are weak at retrospective analysis and that they tend to "beautify" reality when you ask them about their past behavior. I can definitely

ANALYZING RESULTS TOGETHER

Sauli Laitinen, Design Manager, Vaisala, Finland

The goal of user research is to create better products by grounding the design decisions on knowledge about users and usage. User research is also an opportunity to spot potential pitfalls and new design opportunities.

Based on our experience at Vaisala, we can say that user research can live up to these challenges if it is planned and conducted carefully enough. When setting up the user research function at our company, we have learned that it is especially important to pay attention to how research data is analyzed.

One of the first issues we came across was that there is a good reason why textbooks recommend the user-centered design in multidisciplinary teams. On the first projects, we had a good representation from the engineering and user experience departments but lacked dedicated members from the other relevant branches of the organization. For example, we did not have sufficient participation from the marketing and services departments, which not only led to a situation in which engineers and designers were trying to guess what the other people might see in the data but also made the entire user research appear unnecessarily mystic to the people who were not involved in it.

We addressed this situation by having showcase projects and making it a standard practice to map the entire product life cycle before the user research project starts. Based on the product life cycle map, we invite all the relevant stakeholders to the project team. The map also helps us plan research activities together.

Expanding the project team had additional benefits. It turned out to be an excellent way to create buy-in across the organization for both the findings of the research and the innovations made based on it.

In our experience, there is a real risk that without sufficient buy-in, the results of user research will be ignored. Getting the right people involved in analyzing the data and making the key innovations has proven to be a convenient way to overcome the "not invented here" syndrome and to inspire the people who need to act upon the findings.

The analysis and concept creation workshops have also become a natural starting point for new projects. The high-level goals for projects are set during these meetings. From the user experience point of view, this workflow is very encouraging because user research data gets integrated into project goals seamlessly and without extra effort.

Color the experience

Participating in study sessions can be an overwhelming experience for stakeholders: so many things happen and so much important information is discussed or used. A brief eye-blink or a two-second lack of focus from an observer might mean that they miss the most important thing in a one-hour session. One of the most important jobs you have as a moderator of a UX study is to color the experience for observers.

I learned this term "coloring the experience" from my flight instructor way back when I was a cadet in the Air Force academy. Three quick months passed by from the time I was drafted until I was airborne. I flew a very small plane. I was 17 years old and I was extremely ambitious. When the time to fly the plane had come, we flew about an hour each morning in a period of three weeks. The goal was not to learn how to fly, but to show your potential. About 90 percent of the class was to be screened out after this stage. To make a long story short, you read a lot about the plane, you learn a bunch of maneuvers by heart, and then you are expected to demonstrate these maneuvers in the air. For example, after learning by heart the steps you need to take when making a turn, the instructor expects you to demonstrate a turn. Pretty straightforward. When you made a mistake, and I certainly made many of them, the procedure was to quickly summarize what you did wrong (during the maneuver) and move on. This was called "coloring the experience." Later, in the debrief room (on the ground, thankfully), you analyzed your mistakes. The trick was that you clearly remembered your mistakes because you already named them out loud during the flight.

- What goals do users have when they come to our site?

- What did we learn in our usability study?

- What are the biggest obstacles preventing our products from selling?

We can work on only one focus question at a time, so we pick the most important one first. (An experienced team can do two rounds of KJ methods in an hour, allowing them to deal with two important questions.)

Step 2: Organize the group

Get folks together for an hour. We want people from different parts of the organization so that we get their different perspectives.

Step 3: Put opinions (or data) onto sticky notes

Putting one item on each sticky note, we ask each group participant to brainstorm as many items as they can think of.

Step 4: Put sticky notes on the wall

In random order, each participant puts his or her sticky notes up on the wall. Then they read other people's contributions. If, at any time, they think of something else that should go on the wall, they jot it down on a sticky note and add it to the collection.

Step 5: Group similar items

Once everyone has had a chance to add their contributions to the wall, the facilitator instructs the group to start grouping like items in another part of the room. This is what we say when we're facilitating:

> Take two items that seem like they belong together and place them in an empty portion of the wall, at least 2 feet away from any other sticky notes. Then keep moving other like items into that group.

> Feel free to move items into groups other people create. If, when reviewing someone else's group, it doesn't quite make sense to you, please feel free to rearrange the items until the grouping makes sense.

You're to complete this step without any discussion of the sticky notes or the groups. Every item has to be in a group, though there are likely to be a few groups with only one item.

Notice that we've not allowed the group any discussion about the contents yet. We've found that premature discussion often focuses on *borderline* items – things that might be unimportant to the focus question. If they aren't important, then spending any time discussing them is a waste.

Later in the process, we provide time to discuss the important items. Therefore, by preventing conversation now, we save time for the important conversations later.

This step is complete when all the items are moved from the original wall into groups.

Step 6: Naming each group

Using the second color of sticky notes, we ask each participant to assign a name to each group. Here are the instructions we give:

I want you to now give each group a name. Read through each group and write down a name that best represents each group on the new set of sticky notes I just gave you.

A name is a noun cluster, such as "Printer Support Problems." Please refrain from writing entire sentences.

As you read through each group, you may realize that the group really has two themes. Feel free to split those groups up as appropriate.

You may also notice that two groups really share the same theme. In that case, you can feel free to combine the two groups into one.

Please give every group a name. A group can have more than one name. The only time you're excused from giving a group a name is if someone has already used the exact words you had intended to use.

Again, notice that we're not allowing the group to discuss the name. Everyone gets a chance to get his or her own views out, regardless of the politics and personalities involved.

This step has a hidden agenda: the final review. By insisting that everyone read every group, it forces the participants to review and consider everything on the wall. This review is critical for the next step: voting.

Step 7: Voting for the most important groups

When we have finished this step, every participant will have democratically shared his or her opinion on the most important groups, independent of any coercion amongst their peers or factors like the number of items in each group. They'll purely use their own viewpoint to choose those groups that are most important to answering the focus question.

To get through this stage quickly, we break it up into three parts. First, we have each participant grab a piece of scrap paper and write down the names of the three groups that they think are most important.

We repeat the focus question at this point, so they know which question they are answering. For example, if our focus is "What features do users need?" we'll give these instructions to the participants:

> On a piece of scrap paper that you will neither post nor share, I want you to write down the three names of groups that you think best answer this question: What are the most important features that users need?
>
> If a group has more than one name, you are to chose the name that best represents the most important features in that group.

Occasionally, participants will have trouble narrowing the groups to just three. We'll often instruct the people having trouble to write down five, then cross two off. Although this instruction often makes people giggle, it turns out to be helpful to some participants.

The second part of this step happens when they have their three choices. We ask them to rank the choices from most important to least important. We've found that doing this separately from identifying the top three makes it easier on the participants.

After we've ensured that everyone has their three top choices and has ranked them, we give the final instruction: to record their votes on the group sticky notes. If, for example, the group sticky notes were blue, we'd use these instructions:

Go to the blue sticky that best represents your first most important choice and put three Xs on it.

You can then go to your second most important choice and put two Xs on it.

Finally, go to your third most important choice and put a single X on it.

When we're done, everyone will mark six Xs on the group names that they feel are most important.

Again, notice that we've not allowed any group discussion up until this point. Even though they've worked as a group, we've prevented discussion from eating up any portion of the meeting. This is done because, until now, we've not known what items were most important. It just doesn't make sense to spend time discussing unimportant items.

Step 8: Ranking the most important groups

Once everyone has marked their votes, we grab all the group sticky notes with votes on them and place them on the whiteboard (or flipchart). We order them by the number of votes each sticky received, with the highest numbers at the top.

At this point, we ask the group to gather around the whiteboard and we read off, in order of importance, the names of each group that received votes.

Because some groups may actually represent identical priorities, we allow the team a few moments to consider combining groups. We have a simple process for doing this. Here's how we explain it to the participants:

We now need to see if there are any groups that we should combine. You can nominate two groups that you think are the same thing.

We'll then take a preliminary vote to see if anyone thinks they aren't the same. If anyone believes they are different, we'll spend a little time discussing why they believe that.

After the brief discussion, we'll take a final vote. That vote needs to be unanimous for us to combine the items and their scores.

Remember, the two groups being considered need to be identical. That means you could substitute one for the other. A group that's a subset of the other group does not qualify for combining.

As each pair is nominated, we take a preliminary vote. We let the participants discuss amongst themselves why they are for or against combining. We let everyone have their say and pay close attention to the group dynamics to prevent people from getting their opinions bullied.

Because we insist on unanimous agreement for combining items, it gives great power to a single person. However, because the items were already scored, it's hard to abuse the power in any meaningful way. Someone who is trying to hold up the process by being argumentative won't get very far.

Every time we combine two items, their scores are added together and they are moved higher in the list. Usually, we reach a point where there are three or four items that are ranked much higher than the rest. At this point, the facilitator can stop the process, as any further combinations are unlikely to change these top priorities in any meaningful way.

At this point, the facilitator declares the exercise finished and reviews the top three or four ranked items. These are the top priorities for the focus question.

Reaching consensus in record time

When the KJ method works (and it has rarely failed us), we reach group consensus much more quickly than with any other method. Because we've encouraged people from all over the organization to participate, the resulting priorities typically stand the test of time and don't come under constant challenge.

The KJ method is a fascinating mix of independent brainstorming, group dynamics, and democracy. It allows a team to be creative and critical in a productive manner in which strong personalities and politics play second fiddle to the independent perspectives and experience of the team.

The KJ method is such a valuable tool that we sometimes wonder how we'd ever get our job done without it.

Conduct workshops

Workshops are an excellent opportunity for synthesizing observations made in a study and for obtaining team consensus about future actions. Workshops take various shapes and forms. They usually last between one and a few days. Many workshops mostly focus on exercising the KJ method, but there are also other techniques. One workshop I led recently had the following structure:

- 9:00 a.m.–12:00 p.m.: Group work (attendees worked on analyzing and preparing key deliverables from the study).

- 1:00 p.m.–4:00 p.m.: Individual work (each attendee wrote two short pieces – one about an emerging theme from the study, the other more personal, about an interesting experience they have had during the study).

- 4:00 p.m.–5:00 p.m.: Sharing and reviewing each other's work.

I especially favor this structure because it treats stakeholders as equal members of the study team. Yes, people's writing skills are not homogeneous, but I think it is a less critical factor than the collaborated effort. Editing can be done later in the process. In my opinion, creating a feeling of belonging to a learning team that comes up with insights from users is more important than grammar or high level of writing. When a study team is working together on analyzing results, each and every person – be it a product manager or software developer or a UX designer – becomes a champion for acting upon the study recommendations. Other workshop structures might include a couple of days when the team first discusses users and their issues, then identifies emerging themes from the study, and finally comes up with possible action items for product, more research, and design.

There are several guidelines you should consider when you conduct workshops. These should be communicated, discussed, and agreed upon by all workshop attendees and contributors:

- **No email, no phones.** Full attention is required. Build into the agenda several breaks so that people can check on what's happening in the outside world.

- **Lean forward instead of backward.** No wallflowers are allowed; you are there to contribute, play along, and be creative (see figure 4.4).

- **When brainstorming**, no solutions, no judgment of other people's ideas, no censoring your own ideas – but standing on the shoulders of others and developing their ideas is encouraged.

- **Write clearly and concisely.** Whatever you use to write, make sure you use a thick marker pen to write legible, short, crystal-clear ideas. Remember that others need to be able to read them.

The following story from the United Kingdom demonstrates the power of stakeholder workshops. The researcher used personas as a tool for communicating user research findings during a workshop with stakeholders.

USING PERSONAS IN A WORKSHOP TO GET STAKEHOLDER BUY-IN

Amir Dotan, User Experience Architect, Lab49, United Kingdom

While working in 2008 at the Centre for Human-Computer Interaction Design at City University London on an international R&D project called APOSDLE, we were tasked with leading the redesign of the final system prototype. The redesign was to be initiated during a two-day workshop with 21 project partners from across Europe and from diverse professional backgrounds. We knew it was essential to establish a shared understanding among the different partners during the workshop regarding the users' context, needs, and goals. In order to communicate the user information and ensure that everyone in the workshop was on the same page, we chose to use personas to present rich user profiles.

The workshop proved to be a success, as we were able to facilitate discussions that resulted in a new approach to APOSDLE's user interface. Once we introduced the personas, we asked the participants to describe how each persona would likely perceive the current version of APOSDLE. A lively discussion generated considerable insight and helped steer the workshop away from personal preferences and unfounded assumptions. The personas were effective in highlighting apparently obvious attributes such as level of expertise and job seniority that we felt were often lost during previous discussions, which revolved around abstract terms such as "The User" and "The Knowledge Worker."

We instructed our project partners to link any idea they had to at least one persona; otherwise, it was left out. This approach proved very effective and helped keep the discussion focused on the users' needs and context. The personas acted as a constant reminder that APOSDLE's target audience were busy professionals working in a highly social work environment and that they had to constantly acquire and use new knowledge. Overall, though personas are far from a perfect tool, we found them to be extremely useful for the purpose of communicating user research quickly and effectively.

The following story from Germany shows how workshops that are designed to have stakeholders get excited collaboratively about research and design can reduce tension and disagreement within a team and create a fun work environment.

Figure 4.4: UX practitioners and their stakeholders during a workshop held at a Google office in Brazil (printed with permission).

THE POWER OF WORKSHOPS

Jakob Biesterfeldt, Director of International Practice, User Interface Design (UID), Germany

Some time ago, a client wanted our support for a new website. First, we researched user needs and expectations in six countries. We then met with a team of content producers, visual designers, and project managers for two days. We briefly presented the results of our studies, then engaged the client team in the creation of personas and scenarios, designed draft information architecture, and finished with sketching initial interaction concepts.

During and after these two days, we had all project stakeholders engaged, empathetic with the users, and equipped with a common understanding of the content and structure of the new website. We used a variety of creativity methods and lots of visual materials, making the workshop exciting and entertaining. Our clients were happy to be creative, see the research results put into action, and feel connected to the initial website concepts.

Over the next few months, while we completed the website design, there were a few short discussions about these basic concepts. Everyone on the team had a deep understanding of these concepts and why they were what they were. Without such a workshop, I would have expected having to discuss and explain things over and over again, struggling for acceptance every time a new decision was made. Our work would have been less enjoyable and our clients would probably have felt less happy with the result.

Engaging the client in the creation of design solutions is more productive and more fun and will produce better results for everyone.

The next story, coming from Scotland, showcases a participatory design workshop that had a rough beginning and a successful ending.

BUSINESS, MEET USERS . . .

Stephen Denning, User Experience Consultant, Scotland

The value of encouraging stakeholders to work directly with end-users was driven home to me when I was brought into a large UK government department that was almost a year into the redesign of a high-profile internal computer system. It was a complex project environment with separate teams of business analysts, technical architects, designers, and developers across the business and their third-party IT supplier. This structure, coupled with an overbearing government project methodology, meant that progress was slow and inflexible.

It soon became apparent that despite the criticism leveled at the previous system by users, there had been no real attempt at user engagement for this redesign. A methodology requirement to produce some user interface deliverables provided an opportunity to adopt a more user-centric approach under the radar.

Having found some users of the current system who were willing to spare some time to help out, we scheduled a series of day-long workshops, inviting stakeholders from different parts of the project team, along with several users (varying the users in each workshop to keep the feedback fresh). In the first workshop we had two business representatives, two analysts, a technical architect, a designer, the head of the development team, and four users. The first day was tough going, with 12 people in a small room from teams that primarily communicated with each other through documentation!

Maintaining focus was very difficult, and by the end of the day we had little to show for our efforts. However, the next day, with a room change, some coffee on tap, a large whiteboard, and a strict set of ground rules, things started happening. After many weeks of workshops, we managed to examine all of the user journeys for the system. The stakeholders had been able to get firsthand feedback on what was currently going wrong and how it needed to improve, user journeys had been validated, assumptions tested, and – together with the users – some initial screen designs had been created.

> This approach reaped many benefits. Having business stakeholders in atten-
> dance enabled immediate sign-off on decisions, and the technical represen-
> tatives ensured that solutions were technically feasible. Getting everyone into
> the same place at the same time saved time, effort, and cost, and engaging
> the users not only helped to produce a more robust final solution but also
> increased their sense of ownership and buy-in, eventually smoothing the final
> implementation.

Do not report recommendations

When I sense that stakeholders are more likely to implement their own conclusions from study findings, I sometimes choose not to share my recommendations.
Here is a step-by-step description of what I do:

1. I analyze study results and write a report.

2. The report includes only findings. Under each finding, I leave a placeholder
   for a recommendation to be filled in later. Under each finding, I add a title
   that says, "Planned design changes," as well as the phrase to indicate what will
   go in there and when: "Changes will be discussed and determined during the
   next team meeting."

3. I create a separate document in which I list my recommendations.

4. I share the report with the team and invite stakeholders to a meeting. In the
   invite, I ask them to read the report and come up with a list of recommended
   ways to react to the findings.

5. During the meeting, I facilitate a discussion about the main findings. The
   main point is getting possible solutions from team members. The heuristic
   I use is that stakeholders are the ones deciding what should be done. If I see
   that the solution they are getting at is better than what I thought about (which
   happens a lot) or if it is close, then I don't get involved in the decision and
   only provide my support. When I consider the solution they are getting at to be
   wrong, I get involved and offer my recommendation.

I have heard about UX practitioners who don't even get involved in such meetings.
They merely provide a findings report and let others deal with it. Although I see

some advantage in this approach, I think that getting proactively involved increases the chances of somebody actually doing something about what was learned in the research.

 Watch my interview with Aza Raskin, cofounder of Massive Health, who was until recently Creative Lead for Firefox. Previously, he was a founding member of Mozilla Labs. Aza recommends separating the people who find issues from those who identify solutions, and there are many great ways to do that. Use QR code 113 to access the video, a quick summary of the interview, and Aza's biography.

Finally, we'll discuss ways to report results jointly to other stakeholders. Benjamin Franklin once said that we must all hang together, or assuredly, we shall all hang separately. Let's see how you write a report together with stakeholders, present together, and share your gratitude in an honest and public way.

Report results together

When your immediate stakeholders and you together report research results to other stakeholders – possibly including more senior ones – it's hard to argue against the findings. When you and your product manager present together to your manager or to his or her manager, it's a lot more powerful compared to presenting alone. Reporting results together can take many forms, such as a joint report or presentation or an internal blog.

The joint report

I'll discuss reports in further detail in the next chapter. The purpose of this short section is to state how important it is to create a joint report for getting stakeholder buy-in for UX research. When a product manager, a research and development (R&D) manager, a designer, and a researcher appear as the authors of a UX study report, it is much more powerful than having only your name on it. And I don't mean crediting people for work that they weren't a part of. My point is that the people who sign on a report are the ones who were deeply involved in the study planning, execution, or analysis. Needless to say, when a stakeholder signs a report, he or she is more likely to act upon its recommendations.

The joint presentation

When your stakeholders and you collaborate on a UX study, there usually comes a time for presenting the results to others. When that time comes, invite your stakeholders to take an active part. Ask them to brainstorm on the presentation content – its outline, its emphasis, and the stories you will tell. Delegate meaningful chunks of the presentation to them. Ask them what they are comfortable working on and let them work on those parts. Then ask if they are interested in actually presenting these results. If there is one thing I've learned about presenting together, it's that your stakeholders have tremendous persuasion power – a lot more than you have. Imagine that you are communicating about a problem you've observed and that the solution requires allocating significant resources. When you communicate this in a presentation to, let's say, software engineering and product management leaders, it's one thing. When one of *them* presents the same thing, it's much more convincing – especially if that person was deeply involved in the study and is entirely aligned with the recommended course of action. Hence, consider the chunks you hand off to your stakeholders. Don't ask them to talk about who participated in the study or about the methodology. Instead, ask them to present the sensitive stuff. Ask them to talk about the most important findings and suggest the solutions. When they present, provide your full support with spoken and body language (lots of positive nods).

That's powerful stuff. Try it out.

Maintain an internal blog

Earlier in this chapter, I discussed launching a blog for collaboratively documenting Field Friday visits (see the earlier section "Stakeholders in field studies"). You might want to broaden your approach and consider launching an internal blog that covers research studies and findings, inviting stakeholders to participate – read, contribute, and debate. Let every relevant team member have full writing access and do not censor blog posts in any way. Invite stakeholders to comment on your posts as well as on other people's posts. Ask people to post about interesting things they observed during studies, debate controversial results, and add pictures from studies and even video highlight clips. Make it a lively area where people exchange opinions about UX research. Make it everybody's research blog, not yours. Consider it a way of sharing results along with your stakeholders. To make it easier, find at least one person – a software engineering leader or a product manager – who is willing to actively collaborate when you first launch the blog. After things run successfully for a while, invite others to join.

Provide appropriate credits

When people support a study in any way, big or small, publicly thank them. Recognize the importance of their support personally and in front of other people. If you don't provide this recognition, you are unlikely to get help in the future. I provide credit in these three opportunities:

1. **In the report:** I open the report with a list of authors or stakeholders. I finish the report with a thank-you blurb in which I thank each person by name and mention the role they took in the study. For example, "Thanks to Joe Smith (Product Manager) for his support in recruiting participants."

2. **In the presentation:** I open the presentation by saying that this study was a team effort and thank the people who were deeply involved in it. Usually, these are two or three immediate stakeholders. At the end of the presentation, I always have a "Thank you" slide that includes the names of all the people who provided support for the study.

3. **In person:** When I talk with people about a study, I mention the people whose support was meaningful.

I know it's obvious, but people look for recognition. Even if (in your opinion) they are just doing their job by supporting a study, they deserve to be recognized. They expect it. And you, of all people, should be extremely generous with providing this recognition. It's one of the things that help you get more buy-in for UX research, and it's the right thing – and a nice thing – to do.

REFERENCES

IDEO, 2009. Field guide in human-centered design kit. <http://www.ideo.com/images/uploads/hcd_toolkit/IDEO_HCD_FieldGuide_for_download.pdf> (accessed 05.12.11).

Nielsen, J., 2003. 233 tips and tricks for recruiting users as participants in usability studies. <http://www.nngroup.com/reports/tips/recruiting/> (accessed 06.26.11).

Spool, J.M., 2007. Surviving our success: Three radical recommendations. J. Usability Stud. 2 (4), 155–161.

Tullis, T., Albert, B., 2008. Measuring the user experience: Collecting, analyzing, and presenting usability metrics. Morgan Kaufman, Burlington, MA.

TAKEAWAYS

In this chapter, I discussed ideas and techniques for collaborating with stakeholders through user experience studies. I mentioned planning, recruiting, interacting with users, analyzing, and reporting results together. Here are the main points:

1. Identify your organizational UX research uptake based on when you collaborate with stakeholders (see this chapter's introduction), and learn when you should collaborate more to become more successful.

2. Initiate recurring high-level and tactical-level research planning meetings with key stakeholders. Make them short, 30-minute meetings.

3. Obtain ad hoc agreement and buy-in per study. Never skip this step.

4. Work with enterprise users? Collaborate with your company's salespeople. Identify your mutual interests.

5. Start a Field Fridays program.

6. Use the don't-ask-about-future-opinions-ask-about-specific-past-and-current-behavior spiel.

7. During a study session, when something important happens, color the experience for your stakeholders by using body language as well as verbal and written language.

8. Always conduct a field visit debriefing immediately after the session, in the field.

9. Identify and prioritize conclusions and solutions with your stakeholders in meetings and workshops. Don't assume that they will accept your recommendations. Use the KJ method.

10. After you present the study's background and methodology, invite stakeholders to present study results with you.

11. Be kind. Give credit to stakeholders who were deeply involved in research.

CHAPTER 5

The single biggest problem in communication is the illusion that it has taken place[1]

STRATEGIES AND TOOLS TO EFFECTIVELY COMMUNICATE
RESEARCH RESULTS BY USING REPORTS, PRESENTATIONS, AND
MORE COOL STUFF

 twitter 🐦
Arnie Lund

Ok, the deck is done. It's beautiful. An insight on every page. It had better kick influence butt!

[1] GEORGE BERNARD SHAW

Introduction

Reports are important. I don't like them.

Deep down, I understand and appreciate the importance of writing research reports. Written reports add value and have many benefits. They help crystallize the most important things that come up during a study. When you write a report, it makes you think about priorities. It helps you focus on the important things rather than on what very articulate, vocal participants say. When you write a report, you go through a thought process that prepares you for your pitch to stakeholders. Here are some of the benefits of writing a report:

They help create a presentation. After creating a report, it is much easier to come up with a presentation as opposed to starting a presentation from scratch. You just pick the really important things and put them in a slide deck in a coherent, appealing way.

They are useful in the future. Your reports might become useful for others as a resource. Imagine a new product manager joining the team, or a new designer, or the researcher who will take your place one day. Having a written report about past studies is extremely helpful when learning about a product and picking up on a team's knowledge.

You can refer to them professionally. When you are in a meeting, or when you are presenting, or even when you write a different report, it looks professional to refer to a written report. It looks more professional compared to saying something such as, "Remember the study we ran about a year ago? I think we found that people had a problem with the registration work flow."

They contain lots of data. A report is a great format for including large amounts of data, should that be appropriate. For example, a report can always have an appendix that includes the entire study script or tables with raw data. Personally, I prefer to write short reports in most cases, but I do realize that in some situations, it's necessary to include lengthy materials.

They are expected. Like it or not, reports are probably the most popular way to share UX study results with colleagues and clients. This is what people expect, and when you divert from this path without setting expectations, you will be eventually asked to prepare a report.

On the other hand, the fact that everybody does something doesn't mean that's the right thing or the most effective thing to do. I always try to think of ways to report findings in ways that are more compelling than reports. These are the reasons I insist on it:

Writing takes time. Although I have seen people who meet the definition of report writing machines, I cannot complete a report in 24 hours. I need time. After the last user has left the building, I need a couple of days to recover by doing something else. Only then do I begin writing the report.

Nobody reads reports. This is a complaint I hear from many UX practitioners who conduct research. I am extremely familiar with it. I consider myself lucky if three people read any of my reports cover to cover. Most people don't read them; some glance over them quickly. I accept this as a fact of life. I can't make people read my reports.

Reports are static, passive, and silent. Reports are not a format that allows for dynamic, active discussion. They are a piece of paper that someone either reads or not. They might encourage thinking, but they are not a medium that allows for conversation about its content.

Reports have a short shelf life. What happens to a report after it has been read? If the report is a hard copy, it is either shredded or stored in a drawer or cabinet and then thrown away. Its contents are forgotten very quickly. If the report appears in a digital copy, it is either sent as an attachment to an email, or stored in a library within an Intranet site. This destiny is a bit better than that of the hard copy report, in that a digital report can be searched and found, but not ideal.

Readers get lost in the details. It's harder to write short reports than long ones. When you don't limit yourself, you pretty much dump everything you have in the report. You need to make a special effort to come up with a short report that includes only the necessary, important things. Thus, in most cases, people write long reports with lots of details that make it hard for stakeholders to read and sift through.

Reports aren't sexy. Face it, nobody comes to work saying, "Woo hoo, what a great day I am going to have today! I am going to read a report!" (Or do you?)

 Watch my interview with Jared Spool, CEO and Founding Principal at UIE (User Interface Engineering). Jared argues that teams don't need your deliverables: they develop their own. He urges you to ask your stakeholders what they need from you rather than automatically writing a report. Use QR code 116 to access the video, a quick summary of the interview, and Jared's biography.

I realize that many people want to stop writing reports but just can't, for different legitimate reasons. This chapter highlights communication techniques for getting stakeholder buy-in. It provides tips and techniques for improving your reporting and presentation skills, and discusses alternative communication tools and soft skills.

 Watch my interview with Leah Buley, Staff Interaction Designer at Intuit (with Adaptive Path at the time of the interview). Leah says that she has not written a report in a long time. Instead, she produces short video clips and runs end-of-research generative workshops. Use QR code 117 to access the video, a quick summary of the interview, and Leah's biography.

Reports
Avoid the report-which-is-actually-a-presentation

I have seen this result many times and I cannot figure it out. Consultants who have many clients have to give reports in various ways and at various times during a project, depending on the client's wishes. Some clients request a final report in PowerPoint. I have seen this in my career as well. Other researchers I have worked with sometimes choose to prepare PowerPoint reports with slides that contain a lot of information in bullet points. These slides are not meant for usage in actual presentations in front of other people. Rather, they are to be flipped through privately.

To me – and you might disagree – a report is something you read and a presentation is something that accompanies a speaker. The format of a presentation does not work well as a report. It doesn't have a table of contents, it makes you work twice as hard on formatting, and most important, it makes people who actually attend a presentation suffer. Human beings are not good at reading and listening at the same time (Csikszentmihalyi 2004). They first focus on reading from the slide. When they are done reading, the speaker is usually halfway through his or her slide, and then people get bored because they have already read what the speaker is talking about (even the progressive disclosure feature doesn't make things better). At that point, the speaker has lost the audience. Exactly what you want when you talk about research results and action items, right?

When people hear me make these claims, some respond, "Well then, what do you provide to people who can't attend the presentation?" My answer is simple: a report. If you are in a situation where a report and a presentation are required, don't cut corners and create a report-which-is-actually-a-presentation (or a presentation-which-is-actually-a-report, I'm not really sure). Write a report, then prepare a presentation. They are very different ways of communicating research results.

Having said that and also that I don't like to write reports, they are an important aspect of what we do. So let's discuss in detail several report strategies and tactics.

Share key findings before your report is ready

On one hand, stakeholders need quick results. On the other hand, it doesn't usually take 24 hours to complete a study analysis and report. Let's imagine a product manager who needs to make a decision based on the results of a study you are conducting. You planned the study together; you agreed on the goals, questions, and participants; and the product manager even observed a couple of participant sessions. The product manager probably decided what should be done after the study before it was completed. Sometimes she waits for a report. Other times, she will decide to not wait for the report and to make the decision without research input. If that decision contradicts the conclusions of the study you have just completed, you will probably be frustrated. You might even confront the product manager to try to persuade her to wait or change her mind.

There are two effective, appreciated things you can do to avoid these situations altogether. I highly recommend you use both:

Agree on a deadline in advance. In Chapter 2, I mentioned several questions that you should ask your stakeholders when you kick off a research project. One of them was, "When do you need the results?" Assuming that you got an answer or negotiated one, remind your product manager of the agreed-upon deadline throughout the project (during planning, execution, and analysis).

Share findings quickly after data collection. Whether you do that in a meeting or in an email that you send 24 hours after the last participant has left the building, it is extremely effective and important to communicate what you found fast. Maybe you don't have any recommendations and conclusions, but you can collect your main findings and share them with your stakeholders. If they make a decision before the report is ready, at least they can do it based on the findings. I have seen practitioners who tend to share chunks of the yet-to-be-published report with their stakeholders. This approach has two goals: obtaining feedback from the stakeholders and showing them that progress is being made.

One technique that will help you if you are a bit slow to complete reports is writing down one summary paragraph after every participant session. As soon as the session is over, take five minutes and summarize the main findings and participant characteristics. It is hard to do because all you want to do is get your cup of coffee or tea, rest, and get ready for the next session, but the effort is definitely worth it. These paragraph-long summaries have several benefits:

- They will tremendously help you remember what happened during each session.

- Providing proper editing, they can serve as participant descriptions in your final report.

- They can be the things you share with your stakeholders immediately after you complete participant sessions. And by "immediately," I mean five minutes after the last participant session.

One way I use eye-tracking results as a cool communication tool is at that stage between actual data collection with participants and the time the report is ready. I generate visual eye tracking deliverables such as bee-swarm videos, bouncing-ball videos, and heat maps and show them to key stakeholders, describing what they can teach us about our users. As soon as I have something ready, I get up, walk to the stakeholders' desks (or IM them), and ask if they want to see something cool. If they do – and in most cases they do – I invite them to my desk and show them the eye-tracking deliverable. I do that with three to five stakeholders and not necessarily with leaders in the team. Sometimes I'll pick a software engineer who I know will share what they just saw with his or her team. By working from the ground up in this way, I am able to raise interest in the report even before it is ready.

Report structures

You have probably written many standard introduction/method/findings/recommendations reports. This section discusses report organization techniques and the contents of the results and recommendations sections. I have been futzing with my report structures throughout my entire career. I always learn, improve, and adapt. Throughout the years, I have learned that certain structures work for certain people and that these same structures might not be what others expect or are comfortable with.

Organize your report by product areas, problem types, questions, priorities, or tasks

There are different ways to organize the findings and recommendations section in the report. My preferred way to do so is by research questions, but sometimes other organization schemes are more appropriate.

Organize by product areas. Let's assume that you have just finished a study for a content management system including the following main areas:

- **Creation.** Where content items such as articles and videos are created in the system.

- **Approval.** Where content items go through a process of editorial, legal, and executive approvals.

- **Publishing.** Where content items are published on the website after being approved.

- **Reports.** Where various data analytics and metrics about website traffic are generated in a visual way.

- **Admin.** Where access control, approval chains, users, and roles are managed.

Two appropriate situations for organizing your findings and recommendations section by product areas are when findings for different areas are extremely unique and when different development teams work on each area. This way, you are creating a report that is easy for different stakeholders to digest. For example, if there is a dedicated reporting product manager and development team, it is very easy for them to skip all of the sections and jump right in to the report section that is relevant for them. With a different organization scheme, these stakeholders would have to put more time and effort into sifting through findings that are not relevant to them. And because you are in the business of making things easier for people, you might want to prevent this from happening.

Organize by problem types or areas. Sometimes findings logically "belong" to very distinct topics, for instance:

- **Help** (four issues)
- **Quality** (three issues)
- **Lack of system feedback** (six issues)
- **Confusing information architecture** (four issues)

In such a case, it makes a lot of sense to organize a report by these topics.

Organize by priority or severity. When it is extremely important to communicate the hierarchy of issues and the priority of fixing them, reports can be organized so that the most severe problems appear first, then the medium-severity issues, followed by the least severe ones. The disadvantage of this structure is that issues that appear next to one another might be somewhat disconnected, which can make it hard for stakeholders to focus on a problem area.

Organize by study tasks. When tasks are linear or very distinct, it might make sense to organize a report by task. For example, it makes a lot of sense to have report sections for the following study tasks for a content management system:

- Sign up and sign in
- Create a content item
- Approve a content item

- Publish a content item

- View a report about a content item's performance

Organize by research questions. What I have found to be most engaging and effective with my stakeholders throughout the years is organizing a report by the research questions we all agreed upon in advance. With all of the previously mentioned organization techniques, stakeholders might find themselves puzzled with regard to the research questions. In Chapter 3, I discussed the importance of defining a clear set of research questions. When you choose any of the previously mentioned organizational schemes for the report without clearly answering the research questions, you are leaving your stakeholders hanging. Chapters with titles that are identical to research questions make a lot of sense to stakeholders. After each research question title, list both the positive findings and the opportunities for improvements.

Slice reports into digestible nuggets

Some report components are read more than others, and some components are of interest to certain stakeholders but not others. One effective technique for dealing with these facts of life is slicing reports into digestible nuggets. For example, software developers might get a report that includes a short background, a list of things that are working well and are not to be changed, and a checklist of things to be fixed. UX researchers who work with you might get a broader report that includes the full problem analysis, recommendations, and detailed methodology and participants sections.

If you are thinking that I'm being unreasonable here and that coming up with seven versions of one report is not going to happen, ever, Figure 5.1 shows a little twist to this suggestion.

Personalizing the research results for the various stakeholders is key to communicating effectively. When you send a report to stakeholders, indicate the report sections that you think they will find most relevant. For example (using sections from Figure 5.1),

- 3: what we did

- 5: positive findings

Figure 5.1:

Sample report sections.

1 **Executive Summary** ⊞

2 **Goals** ⊞

3 **What we did** ⊞

4 **Participants** ⊞

5 **Positive findings** ⊞

6 **Opportunities for improvement** ⊞

7 **User experience metrics** ⊞

8 **Comparative user experience metrics** ⊞

9 **Research opportunities** ⊞

10 **Appendix** ⊞

11 **Videos & documents** ⊞

- 6: opportunities for improvement

- 11: videos and documents (watch the first three videos)

If necessary, you might prepare seven different report announcement emails. Stakeholders will appreciate that you've thought about what interests them.

Methodology first or last?

Another dilemma for UX practitioners is whether to put the methodology section in the first or last part of the report. A good reason to put it first is that this is what's acceptable in many other research reports and that it is a reasonable, logical place for it. After all, it makes sense to explain what was done, then discuss results. The thing is that methodology sections tend to get long, and by the time your readers finish them, they are exhausted. And they didn't have a chance to read about the study findings and recommendations. That is why many report authors tend to put methodology last. Their line of thinking is that this is not a section stakeholders are interested in and if they really want to read it, they'll find it in the appendix.

Both arguments make sense. What I do in my reports is a compromise between the two approaches. My reports open with a "bottom line" section (the executive summary), followed by a very short "what we did" section (the methodology section). I keep it shorter than 100 words, similar to the length of this paragraph. I pretty much copy the methodology section from the study plan, with some edits (see the section "Selecting a methodology and describing it" in Chapter 3).

THE SINGLE BIGGEST PROBLEM IN COMMUNICATION   CHAPTER 5

Report only the most severe findings

Imagine that you conduct a usability test and come up with 10 positive findings and 50 opportunities for improvement. After analyzing the problems' impact on users, you classify 10 as high-severity opportunities, 15 as medium-severity opportunities, and 25 as low-severity opportunities. It is now time to report your findings. What do you do?

a) Report all 50 opportunities for improvement.

b) Report only the high- and medium-severity opportunities.

c) Report only the high-severity opportunities.

d) It depends.

The correct answer depends on your self-confidence. If you always report lots of findings, it could mean that you aren't confident enough about your results to emphasize the select few that are most important. Every time I see a lot of problems reported, I wish the researcher had shown a bit more confidence. Ask yourself why you would want to report so many problems. Yes, in some situations, reporting all the problems you find is unavoidable. Imagine working in a consultancy for a paying client. The client is hiring your company to find usability problems, and the team that hired you expects you to report everything you find. Other report-all-you-find scenarios happen in regulated industries when you sometimes just have to do it. If you feel some obligation (perhaps even an ethical one) for documenting problems that were found so that someone can dig into these if they want, include a statement about putting the problems in an appendix or auxiliary source.

Let's discuss other situations in which you don't have to report everything. I argue that the less you report, the better the chances that problems are fixed. I report only high-severity problems. The literature offers several severity-rating scales, and it is a popular topic for repeated debate in the UX research community (Wilson & Pernice Coyne 2001; Wilson 1999; Nielsen 1994). I use the following severity scale:

- **High:** Users will not be able to complete the task if the problem is not fixed.

- **Medium:** Users are able to complete the task but are having serious problems.

- **Low:** Users are able to complete the task but are annoyed while doing so.

I try to report only issues that prevent users from completing tasks that they (or the people behind the product they are using) intended to complete. Here is an interesting example: imagine that you've found 12 issues that you classify as low severity. All of them fall under the definition of user interface annoyances such as deleting data that users entered when they come back to an incomplete form or needing to scroll through long pages just to get to a button they need to click, and similar issues. Imagine that four out of six study participants commented that these are so annoying that it makes them want to stop using the product. Can these still be classified as low-severity issues? I don't think so. I think these 12 low-severity issues are actually one high-severity problem with 12 examples. Semantics? Maybe. I believe that if people actually stop using the product, it is a critical problem for the business that's developing it.

In many situations, I have reported many problems with different severities. The thing with low-severity problems is that usually they are easy to fix, and high-severity ones are sometimes hard problems that require many resources. I've seen teams fix 40 low-severity problems claiming that this work highly improved a product while avoiding five critical problems that we were hard to fix.

When research and usability is an integral, frequent part of the development process, I highly suggest that you report only a maximum of 10 high-severity problems per study: no more. This way, you and your stakeholders focus on fixing things that have the most positive impact on the user experience.

The executive summary

The executive summary is a very important tool to get stakeholders' buy-in. Normally, an executive summary is used by stakeholders – sometimes by important stakeholders – to get the gist of what was found and what should be done about it. If the report doesn't include an executive summary or if it includes one that is not written very well, you risk losing the attention of your stakeholders.

To grab your stakeholders' attention, prepare a half-page executive summary (complex studies might require longer summaries) with the following information:

- A short opening paragraph with details about **what** was done, **when**, **where**, **by whom**, and **why**. If the paragraph is shorter than two lines or longer than five, you are doing something wrong.

- A list of three **positive findings**. Choose the three most important positive things that study participants did or said and briefly describe them. Choose only significant positive issues. Otherwise, you are delivering a message that it was hard to find good things to say about the product.

- A list of three **opportunities for improvement**. Choose the three most important things that need to improve, and briefly describe what should be done and why. To help you pick the most significant opportunities, ask yourself what the three things are that if changed would have the highest positive impact on product users.

For a sample executive summary, read Molich's sample usability test report for Tower Records (2010).

There's always the question of how long a report should be. What's too long? What's too short? What's the threshold? Though there is no definitive answer to these questions, the next section provides some insights.

How long should a report be?

The different components included in reports directly affect their length and the chances that your stakeholders will read them. The components you choose to include will probably differ if you are writing a report in a consultancy for a paying client or if you are an in-house practitioner trying to engage the people you work with on a day-to-day basis.

A standard report for most of the research studies should be about five to ten pages long. That number includes any images you choose to add to it, not including a title page. My experience has shown me that longer reports are rarely read and are considered to be a burden on stakeholders. I tend to write reports from five to ten pages long. I never plan the length in advance but I know I should stay within this range.

Here are a couple of exceptions to the rule. If I worked in a consultancy, I would probably align my strong beliefs with what clients expect and write longer reports. I would, however, try to convince everyone involved, including the client, that long does not mean better or more comprehensive or smarter. I would argue

Figure 5.2:

Suggested page count

for short and long

reports.

Report element	Short report	Long report
Title, author, date, stakeholders	Page 1	Page 1
Contents (links to bookmarks in the doc)	Page 1	Page 1
Bottom line (or executive summary)	Page 1	Page 1
What we did	Page 2	Page 2
Why we did it	Page 2	Page 2
Who participated	Page 2	Page 2
What we found	Pages 3–5	Pages 3–10

that longer reports are much easier to write than shorter ones. When you write a short report, you work hard to communicate only what's important. If you, the client, have well-crafted, succinct answers to your research questions, what else do you need? If you have straightforward, actionable recommendations that you can do something about tomorrow morning, why would you need 10,000 more words to back them up? Disclaimer: I refer to product research in a corporate setting. In this context, using lots of words is often a waste. In other organizations, it might be different.

There are situations when you need to write long reports for good reasons. When the FDA asks for a usability study to approve a certain medical device, it needs all the details. In other corporate environments, long reports are less likely to be read.

When the report is ready, don't send it immediately. Be careful not to start unnecessary fires.

Don't start fires

Here's why I recommend not sending your report as soon as it's ready. Sometimes a few of your findings might make people feel uncomfortable. Some will feel that they are being attacked or that their work is being attacked. You might not be aware of the effect your report will have. Thus, it might be a good idea to first share the report with a small number of stakeholders before you make it available to the entire team or to a larger audience. These recipients could be your manager, a colleague you trust, and the immediate stakeholders such as the product manager or the software developer. If there is one specific stakeholder who always pokes holes in your reports, maybe he or she is the one with whom you should share your report first. Let this person find these holes and help you come up with a better report. He or she, in return, will feel appreciated. You both win.

If you find out during these feedback cycles that you have offended someone with something you wrote or included in the report, I suggest doing the following: if the report is not done yet, share the sensitive point with the person who might get offended. Explain that the last thing you want to do is hurt somebody with your reports and apologize. Offer to rephrase or completely remove the points you are about to make public. Offer to work with that person to solve the usability problem confidentially. Consider it an opportunity to closely introduce your expertise to a person who might not be familiar with the UX field. If the person resists your attempts to solve the issue, respect his or her wishes. Do not include this issue in the report. Personally, I prefer to not solve a usability problem rather than solve it but burn bridges. Good things happen when you build rather than destroy bridges.

Use the report as a live communication tool

What usually happens after a report is sent? In most cases, the researcher gives a presentation of the report highlights and often follows up with stakeholders to make sure they act upon findings. And what about the report? Usually it is long gone and forgotten deep in physical or mental drawers a couple of days after it was sent. If you have decided that a report is what's needed (or if nobody really says whether you should write one), it is up to you to make the most out of it. Turn the report into a live communication tool by taking advantage of cloud computing. Use an online word processor (such as Google Docs) and share the report with stakeholders. By adding two simple words ('PM' and 'Eng') after each opportunity for improvement, you turn the report and the negotiation phase that follows it into a transparent process. The findings in my reports include the following:

- A number for easy referencing later on.

- The description of the finding, including a very short analysis explaining why it happened.

- A numbered opportunity for improvement that describes in one or two short sentences what is recommended to fix the problem.

- A placeholder for the product manager's response to the finding and opportunity. I just put "PM:" and color it red.

- A placeholder for the lead software engineer's response to the finding and opportunity. I just put "Eng:" and color it red.

It looks something like this:

---

2. Confusing information architecture, vague terminology

All of the participants could not find what they were looking for by using the navigation bar. The reason was that the terminology used for navigation elements is different from what participants are associating with this type of website. For example, they did not associate the term "Mortgage," which they were looking for, with the term "Loans," which appeared in the navigation bar.

Opportunity 4: change the term "Loans" to "Loans & Mortgages" or consider separating "Mortgages" from "Loans," making it a higher-level navigation element.

PM:

Eng:

Before I share the report with the entire team, I share it with my immediate stakeholders, the product manager and the lead software engineer. I ask them to read it and briefly respond to the findings and opportunities. After they do so, I share the report with the entire team. I then schedule a follow-up meeting with my stakeholders and discuss next steps based on everyone's input.

The next section deals with a popular tool for communicating research results – the presentation. A lot has been said about the art of presenting. This next section describes several techniques that will help you engage your stakeholders with presentations.

Presentations
Learn the art of presenting

Tell a story

Stories are a tremendous tool for delivering UX research findings. In the very few minutes it takes to tell a story, powerful messages can be transferred. Stories have their way of making vague and sometimes boring details of a user experience study into vivid images of situations and what a development team can and should do about them. I highly recommend the excellent book *Storytelling for User Experience* (Quesenbery & Brooks 2010) to get an even better idea of how to collect, create, and use stories effectively in the user experience design process. I'd like to share with you two ways I use stories that I've found to be extremely effective in engaging stakeholders, especially in a presentation setting:

Lightweight storytelling means that during study sessions (a traditional lab study, a field visit, or a phone interview), I always listen for pieces of information that indicate an interesting story behind them. I always ask participants to tell me these stories. Sometimes I directly ask participants to tell me a story. For example, "Tell me about the last time you were really late to an important event or meeting." This last question generates tons of rich data and very interesting stories. Notice that it is not focused on a product or its features; nevertheless, it can be extremely helpful in shaping a list of characteristics of a product, such as a reminder system of some sort. I use these short, sometimes anecdotal, stories during presentations of study results to spice things up. They make findings more real and believable, and they make your stakeholders think about real people and their needs instead of features of a product.

Heavyweight storytelling is not for everyone, although I highly encourage anyone to try it out. Heavyweight storytelling usually involves a field study or a more strategic study, definitely not a study that has a goal of finding usability problems with a certain design. After completing the study sessions (usually visits or interviews), you and the team come up with the emerging themes from the study. At this point, if I think a story is appropriate, I try to write it based on these themes and on what we heard from study participants. Sometimes I write a story per theme if they are big and meaty. I use the composite story (or composite scenario) technique, in which I create a story that combines other told stories. I base the story on what participants said or did while using exaggeration in a way that makes everything happen to a couple of characters in a matter of a couple of days (or less) to better illustrate the findings. Because a composite story might have credibility issues, I tell my audience that the organizations and characters mentioned in the story are fictional and that the situations and things the characters do and say are based on what participants shared during the study.

When I present with a heavyweight story, I usually start with it. I just read it in front of the team. I must say that they usually are very surprised when I do that. But they get the idea and the reasoning behind it as the story progresses. By the time I am done with the story, they are open and ready to hear what I suggest. I usually quickly go over the main messages that the story delivered, then I move on to what we should do about it. And then I open things up for discussion.

Stories work like magic. They make people listen, they are fun, and they are effective. If you can't write stories, the least you can do is collect them from your study participants and share them in creative ways with your stakeholders.

 Watch my interview with Donna Tedesco, a staff usability specialist in the user experience research team at a large organization located in Boston. Donna suggests telling stories using quotes because stakeholders respond well to words that come straight from users' mouths. Use QR code 114 to access the video, a quick summary of the interview, and Donna's biography.

Another technique for engaging stakeholders is using more than words to communicate results.

Make them see, hear, and touch findings

Words on a slide – especially lots of them on one slide – might be shutting your audience off. To open them up and catch their attention with research findings and recommendations, you need to first use fewer words than your intuition guides you to use. Have a good reason for every word you put on a slide, and after you do that, cut the number of words you use even more. To make people engage with your message and want to act upon what you are suggesting, also use visuals, printouts, posters, study artifacts, videos, and audio recordings.

 Watch my interview with Donna Spencer, a freelance information architect, interaction designer, and writer from Australia. Donna says that her primary deliverable is a whiteboard and a marker, which she uses to tell stories to her stakeholders. Use QR code 120 to access the video, a quick summary of the interview, and Donna's biography.

Here are some examples of things that have worked for me in the past:

- Printing out an interesting spreadsheet one participant created to make sense of how certain data works in a certain application. Have a couple of printouts and pass them around during your presentation. Have only a couple of printouts to create suspense among stakeholders.

- Hang a couple of posters to demonstrate main points. People will explore them before the presentation starts, when you point them out during the presentation, and when they are leaving the room.

- A short video of a participant interacting with the evaluated product or being asked a key question. Stop the video at key points and have a short quiz on what people think the participant will do or say next. Then roll the video and compare the results.

- Play an audio recording of an interview segment. I found that people concentrate even more when they listen to an audio recording rather than watch a video.

Sometimes I think there's no wonder we UX people "get it" more than others. We have the advantage of directly interacting with users or potential users of products. Many people in our teams don't have this luxury. The least we can do is bring users to them in any way we can so they can see what users do, hear them out, and experience what we UX people have learned. Words on slides can't create that effect. This is why good true stories are important.

Watch my interview with Ido Mor, Director of Strategic Research at Cheskin Added Value in California. Ido acknowledges that they make PowerPoint presentations for their clients, but they try to make them as experiential as possible. He says that Cheskin is constantly trying to find ways to avoid creating PowerPoint presentations. Use QR code 123 to access the video, a quick summary of the interview, and Ido's biography.

The following story, from Japan, is an example of a reporting method that helps stakeholders get a better feel for study results.

WHY A BOOK MATTERS

Takashi Sasaki, Partner and Consultant, Infield Design, Japan

In today's ever more challenging design practices, a great place to start a project still is – and always will be – observing users in their real lives. But simply observing users is not enough for good design. Worse, we tend to jump from one isolated episode that we've observed to a direct design solution. In order to make the most out of users, we need to carefully synthesize the dots we observed and envision lines, patterns, and shapes that represent an abstract framework for desirable user experiences. Then comes another challenge: sharing our thoughts and ideas with project stakeholders not directly involved, including key decision makers. Vivid impressions from fieldwork and subsequent ideation processes are inherently difficult to share. One way to get our stakeholders equally excited about our achievements is creative documentation, where a book really shines.

A physical book might appear obsolete. We at Infield Design, however, have produced more than ten project books in the past six years, each of which has been greatly appreciated by its client (see figure 5.3). We learned through those experiences that the following two reasons, among others, are why our clients particularly like producing project books:

- Photos, texts, illustrations, diagrams all come in handy. Even a cutting-edge display cannot beat the crisp realization of printed ink on paper, at least for now. Books also have a much friendlier posture than a deck of PowerPoint slides; they can be easily browsed, skimmed, or passed around at a coffee shop.

- It's a great opportunity for all team members to reflect on a project. Producing a book is a lot of work, including prioritizing information, writing and editing texts, preparing photos and sketches, and integrating all materials into actual page layouts. Those activities are indispensable exercises for all team members to reflect on what the team has achieved. We especially encourage client members to write about their fresh impressions, their thoughts, and their ideas. Doing so helps them internalize their project experience and enhances their sense of ownership. When we see our writings appear in a project book, we strongly feel that we are part of a collective achievement. We might go back to the book from time to time. We might passionately talk about the book with others. Even a colleague from a different department might browse the book and become interested. The book will stay alive and will tell its own story.

Figure 5.3: Books prepared by Infield Design, Japan (printed with permission).

Many researchers wonder how they should divide the time within a presentation they are giving. The next section makes some recommendations.

Focus on findings, principles, guidelines, and action items

When preparing a presentation of study results to stakeholder teams, UX practitioners have to balance between types of content that are interesting to themselves and those that are interesting to their stakeholders. I am always torn over this, but I have come to realize and accept that I am not the client here. In a standard study results presentation, stakeholders are mostly interested in what was found and what they should do about it. Everything else is noise to most of them. The two things that are important for them to know before you start with findings and recommendations are the goals of the study (why was it conducted) and the methodology (what you did). As for the latter, I'd like to emphasize that it should be very short: one or two sentences at most. Give the goal and methodology each one slide. As a rule of thumb, the time you allocate to findings and recommendations should be about 10 times more than what you allocate to other topics. For example, if you give a 60-minute presentation, dedicate about 5 minutes to your introduction and about 55 minutes to findings and recommendations, including discussion.

To make your presentation engaging and relevant to stakeholders, carefully develop and discuss findings, design principles, guidelines your audience can follow, and action items. You might think this approach is too direct and even "bossy" – and you might be right. My experience has taught me that telling your stakeholders what you want them to do and why has better results than circling around the problem and hoping they will figure out the obvious thing to do. Your audience is not stupid; they are smart professionals. Be as direct as possible with them while keeping in mind that nothing's personal. You are all there to be successful. You are there to make users successful in achieving their goals with products. Being direct in the way you report findings, recommendations, principles, guidelines, and action items is one of your most important tools. Use it.

 Watch my interview with Aza Raskin, cofounder of Massive Health, who was until recently Creative Lead for Firefox. Previously, he was a founding member of Mozilla Labs. Aza says it is the role of researchers and designers to cross the empathy bridge to stakeholders and to present their findings in a way that is useful for others. Use QR code 113 to access the video, a quick summary of the interview, and Aza's biography.

One proven way of engaging people with the content of a presentation is using pictures. Large pictures. Many pictures. The next section provides some ideas for how to go about that.

Present with pictures

People use slides because they are afraid of forgetting what they need to say during the presentation. I am not going to give you the entire Presentation Zen spiel. I highly recommend you read it (Reynolds 2008; Tufte 2005). That is not to say that you should follow everything they say, but the general idea is as follows. Human beings are not capable of digesting two channels of communication at the same time. We cannot read and listen at the same time. What sadly happens in the vast majority of presentations is that the presenter uses slides with long sentences organized in bullet lists. When slides come up, the presenter turns his or her back to the audience and starts reading to the audience. Because people read faster than the presenter speaks, by the time he or she is halfway through, they are done with the slide. They are now bored because they already know what the speaker is going to talk about, so they forget him or her. After a couple of slides, they just give up and don't even bother listening or reading. Their thoughts start drifting off, they just do other things (smartphones and laptops are great saviors here), or (if they don't have a smartphone) they just fall asleep.

The way I fight this problem is by presenting with pictures and very few words on the slides. Others use charts and pictograms. I use associative pictures to remind me of what I need to say and to entertain my audience so that they are kept interested. I have found that using pictures in slides makes people listen to what I have to say and makes it easier for them to remember what they hear for a long time after the presentation is over. Having said that, not everything can be boiled down to pictures. For example, presenting results from a competitive benchmark might require you to use textual slides.

The following story from eBay features a slide deck that people remembered.

THE ICE CREAM PRESENTATION

Beverly Freeman, Senior User Experience Researcher, eBay, United States

eBay has had two main buying formats (auction-style and Buy It Now) for many years. The idea of dividing the search results page into two columns (one for auction-style and the other for Buy It Now) has been considered. After conducting research that revealed some disadvantages to this approach, the challenge was how to convey the insights in a compelling manner. Inspired by those in the design team who use sketching as a communication tool, I bought myself a digital pen tablet.

The first few slides of my Quest for Ice Cream presentation (see figure 5.4 **A** through **D**) consisted of sketches of a stick figure at "eBay Grocers" seeking a particular flavor of ice cream but instead seeing the frozen food aisles organized not by food type, but rather by calories in one scenario, price in another scenario, and so on. The analogy helped stakeholders understand that this layout might be useful in some situations but may not be the best default view. "The ice cream deck" kind of took a life of its own after that, and to this day people refer to it as such.

(A)

Suppose eBay were a **grocery store**...

... and users came seeking **ice cream**...

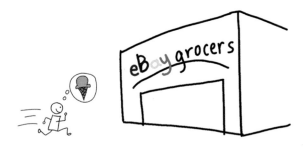

What would be the best way to help them find what they want?

Figure 5.4: Slides from the Quest for Ice Cream presentation (printed with permission).

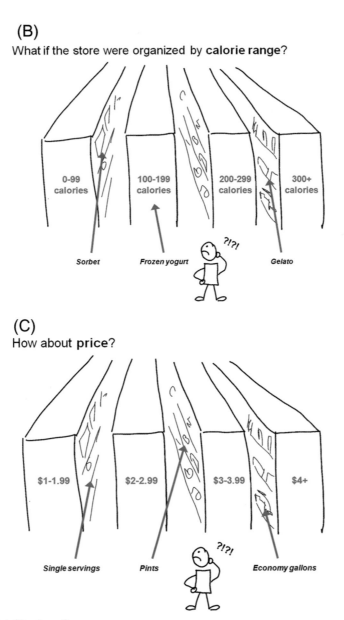

Figure 5.4: (Continued)

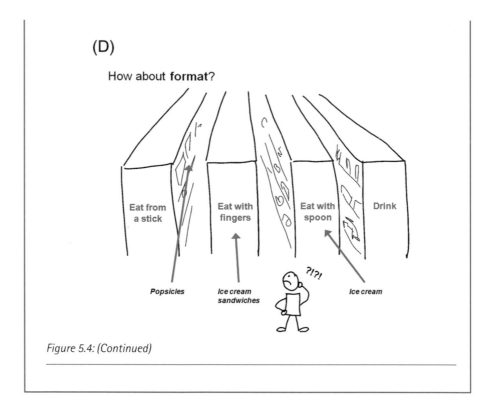

Figure 5.4: (Continued)

Practice, practice, practice

I'm pretty sure it's not breaking news when I say you should always practice giving your presentation. If you can practice more than once, that's great. If you can practice with an audience whom you trust to give you honest feedback, that's awesome. I know all this means you need to step out of your comfort zone, but hey, being brilliant in a presentation causes stakeholders to listen to you. Think about the result you want. Practicing in front of others is a tool for you to get to that result.

What doesn't count as practicing:

- Silently walking through your presentation
- Constantly flipping through your slides
- Closing yourself in a room and mumbling your talk to yourself
- Telling a friend or colleague what you will be talking about

Practicing means you stand up and present while using your voice with the exact things you will say during the presentation. It also means you control the presentation of your slides. You can do it alone or with others as a pretend audience.

Here are the ten steps I go through to practice my presentations. This approach may or may not work for you. I'm including the steps to prepare the presentation because I see them as a part of practicing it:

1. **Sketch.** I brainstorm while sketching ideas on a piece of paper or a whiteboard.

2. **Slides.** I create slides with almost no words – mostly pictures.

3. **Script.** I write down a script for my presentation. I pretty much write down word for word what I want to say during the presentation.

4. **Edit.** I read the script, edit it, and make necessary changes to the slide deck.

5. **Read.** I read the script several times.

6. **Practice 1.** I start by giving the presentation alone and trying not to look at the script. It doesn't really work the first two or three times, so I peek at the script whenever I forget what to say.

7. **Cards.** I grab cards and write down the highlights of my script.

8. **Practice 2.** I practice a few times with the cards, trying not to look at the script. At this point, I usually peek once or twice at the script.

9. **Practice 3.** I practice a few times without the script or the cards.

10. **Relax.** I try not to go over the cards or the script or the deck at least two hours before the actual presentation.

I'm sure you noticed that I violate my own recommendation to give the presentation to a trusted colleague. To be honest, when I do this step, it is highly beneficial. But I find myself avoiding it more than doing it. It makes me feel uncomfortable. You can make your own choice, of course. Again, if you are more comfortable with this step than I am, you will find it extremely helpful.

The art of presenting is also about choosing whom to present to, not just how to present. The next story describes a technique for eliminating stakeholder objections to results during presentations.

Present to Your Biggest Critic

It happened when I was first experimenting with measuring usability metrics in lab studies to support qualitative findings. I was extremely excited about this, and I used to generate many charts that looked very cool (in my humble opinion). When I presented study results to my team, there was always this one software developer who constantly poked holes in my presentation, especially in my cool charts! He did it in front of the entire team and made his points quietly, but sharply. His primary concern was that I presented results in a way that dramatized the actual findings. He claimed that the details of my findings and charts were good enough to present the case for fixing issues. The most annoying thing was that he was always right. And that he said all that in front of everybody I worked with every day. My initial response was to avoid him. I did not want to present anything when he was attending and I did not want to work with him. How dare he humiliate me like that? Today, I laugh at my initial response. I was clearly a very young, inexperienced, unconfident practitioner. I did not have a good working relationship with this guy for a couple of months and it probably affected the user experience of the application that he and his team were working on.

But that's not how the story ended.

At a certain point, I decided to take a step back and reflect on my behavior. Being insulted is a choice, I believe. You choose to take it or not take it to heart. And I initially chose the wrong path. I tried to think of a way to change things for the better . . . and I found it. When the results of my next study were ready and I was about to present them, I asked that developer if he was willing to be the first person to see the presentation and help me make it better. He was happy to do it. We met for an hour and I gave him the presentation as if he were the team and he gave me his feedback. This was great for several reasons:

- He got to provide his feedback and be heard.
- I got to receive feedback and improve the presentation.

- He didn't feel the need to poke holes in my logic and delivery during the team presentation.

- He felt that his opinion counted.

- He was first to see the results.

This preview became a habit for both of us. Each time I was about to give a presentation with research results, I let my biggest critic poke holes in it, privately. But it did not stop there. At a certain point, I thought he could be a real champion for UX research in the team and company. I wanted him to experience more than what usability testing has to offer. When the right opportunity presented itself, I invited him to join me in a large-scale international field study. During one of the preparation meetings for this study, he suddenly looked at me and said, "Wow, I didn't realize that UX research involves so much thought, methodology, and detail!" That moment was when I knew he had become a UX research champion.

Present to multiple teams

Usually, there is one team or a couple of people who are (or should be) interested in the results of a UX study. These are the immediate stakeholders. They are the most important people to get buy-in from because they can change the design based on research results. But there are many other peripheral teams that might be interested. Some should be extremely interested. It is your job to share the results of UX studies with these teams – especially if you'd like to make a positive impact with your research. Here are two examples.

When I try to answer research questions related to a variety of aspects of a product, it is a great opportunity to share the results with multiple teams. I once studied the experience of getting help through context help "bubbles" and through the main help area of a product that I was supporting. I found many interesting things and had a bunch of recommendations to improve our Help approach. I shared the results with my immediate stakeholders. I also shared them with product managers who oversaw other products our company developed. I shared them with our technical writing group and with software developers who sometimes wrote help-related content on their own. I believe that this approach helped create better products and increased awareness to what UX research brings to the table.

When I conducted my first eye-tracking study, it was the first time it was done in my team for a product that was planned and developed for a long time by many people worldwide. The study had very specific goals and was intended to fine-tune a design by learning about what elements users fixate on and how they scan certain pages. The immediate stakeholders were the designers of the product. During the preparation of this study, I realized that there was a lot of interest from the team. Product managers, software developers, salespeople, and technical support staff were all interested in the study and were anxious to see the results. When the analysis was done, I first wrote a report and shared it with the design team. We had follow-up meetings during which we agreed on next steps. Next, I crafted a presentation that was ten minutes long. It included two slides with the study background and about ten slides with the eye-tracking results. Each results slide included a brief text (not more than ten words) that described a certain conclusion and a large visual, primarily a heat map or an area-of-interest chart. I gave this presentation during weekly team meetings of the product management team, the software engineering team, technical support, services, and sales. I talked for ten minutes and took questions for about ten more minutes. It was amazing to see how different people were so interested in these results for different reasons. Salespeople and product managers began using one of the heat maps in their pitches to new and existing clients to demonstrate how seriously our company takes user experience design.

One more reason for giving a results presentation to multiple teams is the opportunity it carries for you to practice. If there is one specific team that is more important for you to persuade with your findings and recommendations, first present to teams that are more peripheral and in less immediate need of the results. This way you get to sharpen your slide deck and presentation based on your experience and people's response and comments.

Although reports and presentations are probably the most popular communication methods for UX research results, other tools and techniques are also extremely effective. The next section introduces and discusses their characteristics and usage.

Other communication tools and techniques

Videos

Video highlight clips can be powerful and highly effective. They work especially well when you deal with stakeholders who have no time or patience and ones who have what I call a "SQUIRREL disorder." People with a SQUIRREL disorder have a hard time focusing on one thing at a time. Use QR code 141 to access a YouTube video that demonstrates the SQUIRREL disorder. If you have a stakeholder who suffers from a SQUIRREL disorder, I recommend communicating findings with short highlight clips. These videos will grab their attention. They will be their squirrels.

I asked Chris Hass, an esteemed colleague, to share his experience and knowledge of best practices for creating a highlight clip. If you are thinking of creating a highlight clip or have been creating them for a while, Chris has great advice for you.

THE MOST POWERFUL TWO TO TEN MINUTES OF YOUR RESEARCH FINDINGS PRESENTATION

Chris Hass, Senior Vice President Experience Design, Mad*Pow, United States

Nothing convinces a recalcitrant team (or CEO) that change must happen like video clips of study participants. Two minutes of the right video clips can instantly realign team politics, philosophies, and agendas into harmonies so sweet you could sing them. Video is the nuclear bomb of change making. But why?

If you've planned your research with the client and their stakeholders; if your research plan is unbiased and repeatable; if your recruitment screener and moderator's guide were well conceived and everyone that matters had signed off on them; if your research execution was unbiased and professional; if your data and conclusions can withstand unflinching scrutiny – and they certainly should be able to – then your findings should be objective. Truthful. Unassailable.

And nothing illustrates unassailability like video. Why? Your clients and colleagues might trust you. They might trust the process. They might trust the findings. They will always trust their eyes. However, there's a catch: video is a lie. Once you turn 8 (or 80) hours of video into 10 minutes of salient, representative clips, you are reporting, editorializing, or both. Clip selection defines the impact your findings will have. What moments best support your conclusions? (Reporting.) What will move clients towards change? (Editorializing.) It's your responsibility to ensure that clips fairly represent what happened during the research and why it's important.

Here are some tips for making clips that convince:

- **Pick key moments:** Which best represent key findings? Which solve team struggles? Are they witty, trenchant, or funny?

- **Recognize the limitations:** Presentations often happen in conference rooms with no sound systems or speakers. Choose representative moments that can be quickly understood and easily heard. Bring speakers.

- **Give viewers time:** It can take 5 to 10 seconds – and sometimes longer – to attune to a video clip. Insert appropriate pauses before and after clips.

- **Caption it and recap it:** Before showing a video, describe what the clips contain and their relevance. Add a summary caption under the video window or use captioning software. Afterward, briefly restate their importance.

- **Begin and end on a positive note:** The best final clip is a user saying, "There's much work to be done, but with some effort it could really be great. I'd be proud to use it."

Don't underestimate the power of video. Present your study findings, support them with video clips, and watch consensus build.

Watch my interview with Caroline Jarrett, an independent usability consultant from the United Kingdom. Caroline indicates that a deliverable that works best for her is finding the stakeholder whose job is to align what they do with UX and getting that stakeholder to actually have the experience in some way, whether video or role-playing. Use QR code 122 to access the video, a quick summary of the interview, and Caroline's biography.

Visualize and design posters

Most people are more attracted to exploring information that is presented to them graphically rather than in written words. I have seen this time and time again. People are more engaged by a chart than by a two-page condensed document that describes the information in the same chart. Visualizations of research findings or recommendations are especially useful in the following activities:

- **Brainstorming sessions:** Visualizations help participants come up with more ideas.

- **Interaction design and participatory design:** The visibility of posters with research findings makes them helpful and relevant when designing products with and for users.

- **Use cases:** Nothing boosts the communicativeness of a wordy use case better than a picture, drawing, or sketch.

- **Work flows, decision trees, rich maps, and storyboards:** These deliverables all benefit highly from a visual aspect.

When communicating research findings, I found that posters have a special power. A1-size posters are especially effective (33 × 23 inches, 84 × 59 cm). If done right (i.e., professionally designed), they are a great tool for communicating results, encouraging discussion, and persuading stakeholders to fix things.

Watch my interview with Paul Adams, a product manager at Facebook and former UX Researcher. Paul says that he is a big fan of physical artifacts as research deliverables. He designs huge posters with many details and put them in places where stakeholders hang out. Use QR code 112 to access the video, a quick summary of the interview, and Paul's biography.

I have asked a few of my colleagues to share examples of visualizations they created to engage their stakeholders. I specifically asked them to share those that have been most successful at achieving this goal. The following examples show you the results.

 Watch the video contributed by Amberlight Partners from the United Kingdom. One of the ideas they use to make sure they communicate their ideas and concepts as clearly as possible is illustration. The video features the work of a UX illustrator before, during, and after the research process. Use QR code 137 to access the video, a summary of it, and a short description of Amberlight Partners.

VISUAL THINKING AND COMMUNICATION

Filip Healy, Director of Consulting, and Roland Stahel, User Experience Illustrator, Amberlight Partners, United Kingdom

Hiring a professional illustrator or visual thinker can help communicate concepts, ideas, scenarios, and user requirements more effectively throughout a research project. Figures 5.5 through 5.10 showcase how we use illustration as an integral part of UX processes.

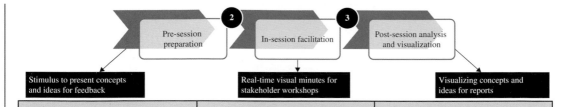

| | **2** | | **3** | |
| Pre-session preparation | | In-session facilitation | | Post-session analysis and visualization |

| Stimulus to present concepts and ideas for feedback | Real-time visual minutes for stakeholder workshops | Visualizing concepts and ideas for reports |

Figure 5.5: Visual stimulus

Figure 5.6: Visual meeting minutes

Figure 5.7: Visual concept

"We have four concepts for our new mobile app and we want feedback from users. Can you run a focus group and ask them?" We can do better. We'll quickly sketch out illustrations to visualize the concepts.

"We need to get our management team in and find out what they want. Can you moderate that?" Yes, and we will use an illustrator to visualize their goals and requirements so that we are all on the same page.

"Can you tell me what users want from my service?" Better yet: we'll sketch out some scenarios and illustrations so you can explain it to the rest of your team.

| Visual stimulus for collaborative activities | Assisting users visualize their ideas in co-creation | Visualizing user journeys and scenarios |

Figure 5.8: Visual stimulus

Figure 5.9: Visualizer

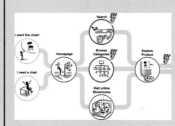

Figure 5.10: User journey

"What text labels shall we put on the cards for our card sorting exercise?" We can add illustrations to ensure that users understand the meanings and get suggestions for better labels.

"We want to do co-creation, but last time our designers laughed at the users' outputs!" We'll bring an illustrator to help the users express themselves more clearly.

"I read the report, but I'm not clear on which findings are the most important and why?" Fair point; here's a picture of your entire user experience and where the major issues are occurring.

USER EXPERIENCE MAPPING

Filip Healy, Director of Consulting, and Roland Stahel, User Experience Illustrator, Amberlight Partners, United Kingdom

In order to enhance our ability to communicate our research insights, we often use visual materials to illustrate ideas, processes, or concepts. One way we do this is quickly create a compelling high-level overview or "map" of the user experience that we are analyzing. This can be a user journey through a retailer website (as in the example in Figure 5.11), the journey a voicemail message makes between the sender and the receiver, or it can just be a set of areas or themes shown visually. The idea is to clearly communicate what is important, efficiently and with impact. The UX map:

- Shows the end-to-end user journey of what the research focused on or even beyond

- Provides context and identifies where pain points occur as well as other useful information

- Helps clients visualize what is happening and engage with the key messages

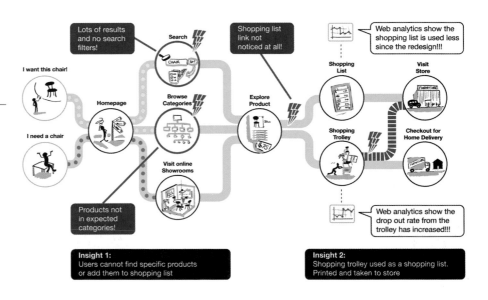

Figure 5.11: A UX map by Amberlight Partners (printed with permission).

- Provides a framework that helps the organization communicate the user experience

- Can show different user types or journeys and requirements across different channels

- Provides a flexible story (rather than starting on slide 1, we can decide where our interest lies)

- Can be printed large to create compelling posters

- Can be interactive to allow interested parties to click through (on digital versions)

Why a map?

We use the term "map" deliberately, as the aim is to help clients navigate the UX terrain. Maps have been around for centuries, and we can use some of their principles to aid our own communication:

- Maps have landmarks; similarly, we have clearly defined stages or areas in our UX maps.

- Direction, distance, and communication routes relate places on maps to each other; similarly, we try to clearly show important relationships such as sequence or causality.

Maps allow their users to see the entire picture of where they are going before selecting the most appropriate route (you may know the feeling you sometimes get from in-car navigation that just gives one instruction at a time with no overall context!). Similarly, we "map" all of the research findings onto the UX map, providing the big picture, which helps users understand the details better.

VISUAL SURVEY RESULTS

Bob Thomas, Manager of User Experience, Liberty Mutual, United States

We're often asked in our jobs as UX professionals to find all the usability issues with a particular application. But I prefer simpler solutions, concentrating on the biggest issues. If our stakeholders can walk away from a presentation on usability findings with the top five issues, and still be talking about them a week later, then I consider our job a success. And because I work for a data-driven company, our key stakeholders are persuaded by data and, more specifically, by data that tells a story.

I recently ran a usability test of three new home page designs. We created three well-designed concepts for the test, each with different layouts and each encouraging the user to interact with it in different ways. The order in which the designs were presented to test participants was counterbalanced. After we gathered qualitative feedback on each design, we asked participants to complete a survey of 25 questions, constructed on a Likert scale from 1 (strongly disagree) to 5 (strongly agree). These questions were focused on such areas as visual design, navigation, content, and efficiency. Our participants completed a survey for each of the three designs.

In a technique I learned from Chris Hass while at the Bentley University Design and Usability Center, I used Microsoft Excel to enter the survey data, conditionally formatting cells so that survey results displayed red for negative results (a Likert score of 1 or 2), yellow for neutral results (a Likert score of 3), and green for positive results (a Likert score of 4 or 5). In other words, green is good and red is bad.

The tabulated Excel spreadsheet can paint an instant picture for stakeholders, in this case reactions of users to the three designs we were considering for our home page. In my usability presentation to stakeholders, I simply opened with three slides showing the survey results from the three home page designs, as shown in Figures 5.12 through 5.14. Although I had another 20 slides in my deck, I didn't really need them to persuade management which design we should go with. The data told the story and sold the solution.

	P1	P2	P3	P4	P5	P6	P7	P8	P9	P10	P11	P12	P13	P14	P15	P16	P17	P18	P19	Average
The overall site is attractive.																				4.4
The site's graphics are pleasing.																				4.4
The site has a good balance of graphics versus text.																				4.2
The colors used throughout the site are attractive.																				4.4
The text (lettering, headings, titles) is easy to see and read.																				4.5
The content makes me want to explore further.																				4.3
It is easy to find my way around the site.																				4.4
I can get to information quickly.																				4.3
It is fun to explore the site.																				3.9
It is easy to remember where to find things.																				4.4
Information is easy to read.																				4.4
Information is written in a a way that speaks to me.																				4.4
Screens have the right amount of information.																				4.5
The site effectively communicates the company's identity.																				4.3
The information is relevant to my needs.																				4.5
The site is designed for people like me.																				4.3
The site's content interests me.																				4.4
The site has characteristics that make it especially appealing.																				4.4
The site reflects leading edge design.																				3.9
The site is exciting.																				3.8
The site is well-suited to first-time visitors.																				4.4
The site is well-suited to repeat visitors.																				4.5
The site has a clear purpose.																				4.6
I always know what I could do next.																				4.0
It is clear how screen elements (e.g., pop-ups, scrolling lists, menu options, etc.) work.																				4.0
Average	4.88	4.68	4.44	3.48	4.56	4.20	3.87	4.60	4.96	4.20	5.00	4.60	4.84	4.08	1.88	4.68	4.04	4.64	4.20	4.3

Figure 5.12: Survey results for design A (home page 1) (printed with permission).

	P1	P2	P3	P4	P5	P6	P7	P8	P9	P10	P11	P12	P13	P14	P15	P16	P17	P18	P19	Average
The overall site is attractive.																				3.6
The site's graphics are pleasing.																				3.5
The site has a good balance of graphics versus text.																				3.5
The colors used throughout the site are attractive.																				4.1
The text (lettering, headings, titles) is easy to see and read.																				3.9
The content makes me want to explore further.																				3.7
It is easy to find my way around the site.																				3.7
I can get to information quickly.																				3.8
It is fun to explore the site.																				2.9
It is easy to remember where to find things.																				3.5
Information is easy to read.																				3.8
Information is written in a a way that speaks to me.																				3.8
Screens have the right amount of information.																				3.8
The site effectively communicates the company's identity.																				3.3
The information is relevant to my needs.																				4.1
The site is designed for people like me.																				3.5
The site's content interests me.																				3.7
The site has characteristics that make it especially appealing.																				3.4
The site reflects leading edge design.																				2.8
The site is exciting.																				2.8
The site is well-suited to first-time visitors.																				3.7
The site is well-suited to repeat visitors.																				3.7
The site has a clear purpose.																				3.8
I always know what I could do next.																				3.5
It is clear how screen elements (e.g., pop-ups, scrolling lists, menu options, etc.) work.																				3.7
Average	3.56	4.48	1.44	3.96	3.44	4.00	3.83	4.36	2.96	4.00	4.56	3.04	4.24	4.48	2.92	3.48	3.20	3.29	3.16	3.6

Figure 5.13: Survey results for design B (home page 2) (printed with permission).

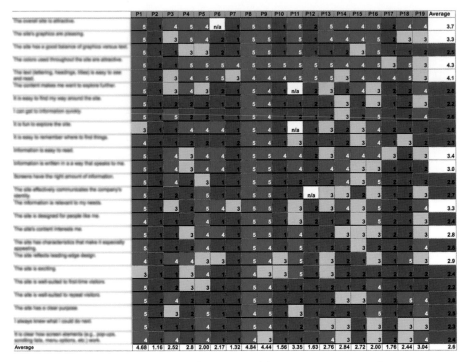

Figure 5.14: Survey results for design C (home page 3) (printed with permission).

PRODUCT CONCEPT BROCHURE

Sauli Laitinen, Design Manager, Vaisala, Finland

At Vaisala, we have found product concepts to be an efficient and effective way to communicate the results of user research. Experience has taught us that it is often better to show a sample solution rather than list the product issues.

Most often, we present the product concepts as five- to fifteen-page marketing brochures. On the cover of the brochure, we have a picture of the product in use. This is followed by a one-page summary of what the product is all about. The bulk of the brochure is dedicated to the storyboard that illustrates the key features of the product and how it is used (see figure 5.15). After that, the relevant technology, architecture, and business information is presented in visual format. The brochures are printed out professionally and handed over in person to the project stakeholders.

Based on our experience, product concepts are not only useful when communicating the results of user research in the beginning of the project, but also help keep key findings fresh in mind at later stages of the development process.

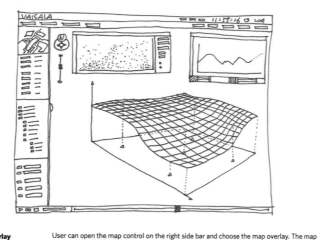

3D map overlay   User can open the map control on the right side bar and choose the map overlay. The map
                            overlay can visualize the   ,   , or others in 3D animations.
                            Playback function helps user to review the   .

Figure 5.15: A sample page from a product concept brochure project (printed with permission).

VISUALIZING KEY DIFFERENCES IN FINDINGS

Michael Hawley, Chief Design Officer, Mad*Pow, United States

Frequently, researchers need to communicate findings that show the differences between several entities – personas, competitor sites, effectiveness of design concepts, and so on. Describing these differences with words is tedious and a challenge for audiences to read. Polar displays (a.k.a. radar or spider diagrams) overcome this challenge by visually communicating differences across several dimensions in an easy-to-scan diagram.

Start by defining spokes as key dimensions for comparison. Then label each spoke with the opposite end of the spectrum for that criterion (see figure 5.16).

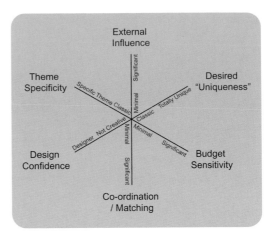

Figure 5.16: Labeled polar display (printed with permission).

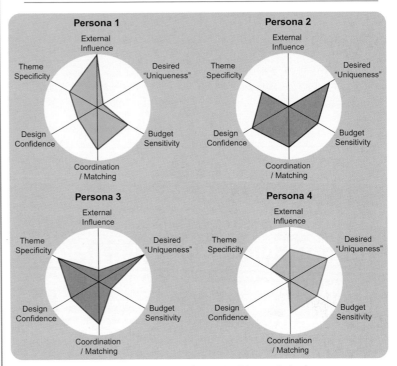

Figure 5.17: Polar displays of personas (printed with permission).

Then, for each entity (persona, etc.), score the selected competitor sites along the various dimensions based on the research and plot them visually. The resulting diagrams help audiences see differences with minimal reading (see figure 5.17).

Finally, here is my own example of a visualization I used and found to work very well with stakeholders.

The Top Ten Themes Poster

After a large-scale field study, a team of two researchers and a designer analyzed the themes that emerged and summed them up in a single poster. Each theme included the following components:

- A short title

- An illustration

- A description of the theme

- The design implications

The poster (see figure 5.18) was used to spark discussions and debate and copies of it were printed and given to relevant stakeholders. Two years after the study, the poster is still proudly hung in the team working area and references to it are still being made in design meetings.

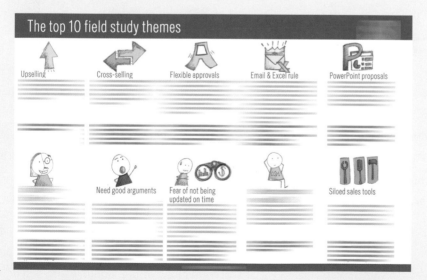

Figure 5.18: Top ten field study themes poster (some of the text was blurred for confidentiality) (printed with permission).

Visualizations and posters are key elements of another effective communication tool: the expo.

Run a research expo

A research expo is a full-day event during which stakeholders *experience* research instead of reading about it. I came up with the idea of having an expo as a communication tool after concluding a field study with the goals of defining strategy around a certain product, learning more about its users, and testing preliminary design concepts. Data collection took place in several countries and involved contextual observation, interviews, and an artifact walk-through. Participants were also asked to keep a diary to share their experiences on a daily basis. The study team included two UX researchers, an interaction designer, a product manager, and the lead software engineer.

The field study produced a large number of insightful findings that we needed to communicate to our stakeholders. However, because we had not previously conducted fieldwork for these particular stakeholders, there was uncertainty surrounding the value and substance of the research. Additionally, we were unsure how the stakeholders processed information or utilized research findings. We also wished to promote and demonstrate the value of field studies to other organizations such as support, sales, product management, and engineering.

Fearful that we might end up writing a report that would get passed over, we decided to try the new idea of holding an expo at which stakeholders could "experience" the research instead of reading about it. We imagined a large meeting room with a self-guided exhibition of posters, artifacts, and videos inviting stakeholders to learn about our results. We planned to conduct this expo for a full day, during which the study team was available to discuss research findings and recommendations with the extended team.

Preparing the expo. During the preparation phase, we brainstormed the contents of the expo and developed a "mind map" of findings. We recruited a designer, who created visual representations of our findings and helped us design several posters for the expo. Posters included:

- Study background

- What is a field study?

- Methodology

- Participant map

- Task work flow

- Participant quotes

- Themes with product implications (see Figure 5.18)

Representative artifacts gathered from participants were selected to showcase. Insightful entries from the incident diaries were also included. In addition, edited video clips from the study sessions were set up in viewing stations around the expo room. A slideshow was produced and included the following topics:

- Research questions

- Process work flow

- Tools and systems users use

- Task matrix

- Top ten issues that mess up a certain process

- Who is the product for?

- Pictures of participants

- Artifacts

   Holding the expo. We created a multimedia experience and set up the room like a gallery exhibit, including video viewing stations (to watch select user clips), posters illustrating key findings and product implications, printed blog posts (participants' diary entries), collected artifacts that people could pick up and discuss, and a slideshow that ran in a continuous loop in the room (see Figure 5.19). During the expo, we (the researchers), the product manager, and the lead engineer answered questions about findings, encouraged discussions about the meaning of the findings, and shared our field study experience.

After the expo, we provided copies of the posters to the product manager, engineering director, and product management director. The following week, we gave presentations to those stakeholders who were unable to attend the expo.

   The website. Using all the content we had prepared for the expo, we created an internal website that was launched on the morning of the expo. The site served as a repository of artifacts, diary entries, videos, and notes from the study. This interactive "report" pretty much wrote itself, thanks to all the expo preparation.

Figure 5.19: The expo room. Projected presentation, posters, video stations (laptops), and artifacts (arranged on table) (printed with permission).

The website was easily discoverable through an intranet search, provided an engaging presentation format, and directly linked the report to the project site.

Outcomes and lessons learned. The results of the expo exceeded our expectations. Approximately 50 people attended the expo, and more than 100 visited the expo website. It's highly doubtful that this many people would have taken the time to read a standard research report. Product managers, engineers, sales representatives, support staff, and UX researchers and designers visited the room throughout the day, watching video clips, discussing the artifacts, and intensely debating the study findings and their implications (see Figure 5.20).

The chief benefits of holding an expo included creating a high level of engagement, rendering study results more memorable, raising the profile and impact of UX research, and increasing acceptance for field studies. Reflecting on this effort, expo attendees still utilized findings and recommendations from this study – even two years after it was conducted – and our team members ask for more studies with similar deliverables. The expo helped us to better appreciate the power of face-to-

Figure 5.20: Stakeholders interact with expo materials (printed with permission).

face interaction with our stakeholders. Facing so many tangible findings in an expo setting made our stakeholders engage with the study results and recommendations.

We found that presenting findings via an expo "democratized" the experience because attendees were more willing to ask questions and engage with the material. This participation is less likely during traditional report presentations, which are often dominated by lead product managers and one or two vocal participants. As a result, many more ideas were generated from a wider group of people. Additional lessons we learned included:

- Consider giving visitors something to take away (for example, a handout of key findings).

- Promotion and marketing is key to a good turnout.

- It pays to include stakeholders as part of the study team.

- Having a great designer is necessary to create strong posters, presentations, and an inviting overall expo experience.

- Including a multimedia component was very conducive to engagement.

Watch my interview with Cennydd Bowles, interaction and UX designer from the United Kingdom and author of *Undercover User Experience Design* and *Designing the Wider Web*. Cennydd says that we, the UX people, rely too much on the big reports and on formal documentation of our work. He argues that disruptive research should be communicated disruptively. His number-one deliverable is not creating a deliverable. Use QR code 118 to access the video, a quick summary of the interview, and Cennydd's biography.

The recipe for an expo, like any recipe, can be tweaked and adapted by the chef to match the nature of the research being reported and the stakeholders involved. The important point is that rich reporting is an improvement beyond the traditional written report, leading to a more meaningful engagement among a wider variety of stakeholders.

When presenting research results to stakeholders, whether as a part of an expo or not, one extremely effective tool is combining quantitative and qualitative data.

Combine quantitative and qualitative data

In Chapter 3, I discussed the magic of injecting quantitative data into qualitative findings. The context of communicating study results is an excellent way to demonstrate this practice. When I plan a traditional lab usability study involving tasks that participants are asked to complete, I come up with a set of usability metrics that add value to qualitative findings. I usually – but not always – measure task success, number and type of errors, satisfaction (per task and posttest), and lostness.

Lostness

Lostness is a usability metric that indicates how lost people are when they attempt to complete a given task (Tullis & Albert 2008). It is calculated based on the following three parameters:

- The minimum number of pages that must be visited to complete the task (R)

- The number of different pages actually visited while completing the task (N)

- The number of pages visited while completing the task, counting revisits to the same page (S)

For example, imagine a task that can be completed by accessing a home page and then an inner page, so the minimum number of pages to complete is 2. When a user tries to complete the task, she accesses the home page, then the inner page, then back to the home page, and back to the inner page to complete the task. That gives us a value of 2 for the number of pages that were visited, and a value of 4 counting revisits to the same page. If you put all these values in the formula shown in figure 5.21 for calculating lostness, you get a score of 0.5.

$$L = \sqrt{\left(\frac{N}{S} - 1\right)^2 + \left(\frac{R}{N} - 1\right)^2}$$

Figure 5.21: The lostness formula (Tullis & Albert 2008).

Lostness scores run from 0 to 1. The higher the score, the more lost a user is. If you sit next to a person attempting to complete a task, you can see with your own eyes that he or she is lost for scores higher than 0.4.

I have found the lostness score to be one of the most engaging things I present to stakeholders. They just love it.

After I run the study and analyze the qualitative and quantitative results, there are two ways to present the data (in a report or presentation):

Separate quantitative metrics from qualitative findings. In the past, I used to have a section called "Findings and Recommendations" followed by a section called "User Experience Metrics" in which I presented charts and analysis for the metrics I measured. If I was utilizing these same metrics in previous studies, I added a section called "Comparative User Experience Metrics" in which I compared results measured in this study with results from past studies to show trends.

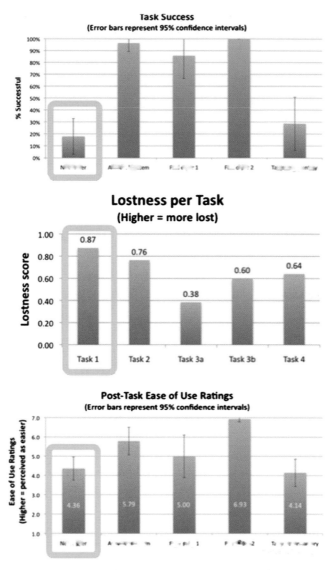

Figure 5.22: Data to support qualitative findings.

Integrate qualitative and quantitative findings by telling compelling stories.
After realizing that many stakeholders are not reading the one or two added
sections with quantitative analysis (mentioned previously), I started communicating qualitative and quantitative results together in a more integrated way.
For example:

When attempting to create a new user role, most participants had trouble choosing
an appropriate user type. Many of them spent a considerable amount of time trying

to figure out the different types, and still got it wrong. A few participants didn't even hesitate when they picked wrong user types. They just moved on.

When integrating quantitative data to support this type of qualitative finding, I add the following:

When attempting to create a new user role, participants were unsuccessful, extremely lost, and thought it was hard to complete:

1.   19% (±13%) success rate

2.   0.9 lostness score

3.   4.4 (±0.6) out of 7 ease-of-use rating

I also add the charts shown in Figure 5.22 to demonstrate the numbers I use and how they compare to other tasks.

My experience tells me that when I integrate quantitative findings with qualitative findings, my stakeholders pay more attention. To them, the numbers are "hard" facts and the stories and quotes are "soft." Together, they make a compelling case for highlighting an issue and pitching its fix.

The next section introduces another effective communication tool you can implement with your stakeholders: a top ten list.

Develop top ten lists

Top ten lists are great for communicating research-based issues with a product. You can develop top ten lists of opportunities for improvement, positive findings, findings per quarter or year, or research-based ideas that require further exploration. Typically, a top ten list of opportunities for improvement include the following in a spreadsheet format:

1.   **Opportunity status:** Use one of three values: No progress, In progress, and Done. I highlight the background of the status with red, green, and blue, respectively. I don't use a red-orange-green color code because this will mean that stakeholders will probably see only red and orange most of the time. I'm trying to remain positive by using green for "in progress."

2.   **Opportunity title:** Short, specific, and actionable.

3.   **Details:** Describe the opportunity in a couple of sentences and provide a suggested or agreed-upon solution.

4. **Product management and engineering owners:** These are the people who need to agree to act upon the opportunity. They are the primary stakeholders.

5. **Affected users:** Sometimes an opportunity is relevant for only a certain type of users, not for another.

6. **Resources:** Indicate the resource of the opportunity (which study, link to report, etc.).

Top ten lists are a great tool for communicating with stakeholders, especially direct ones (such as product managers) and executives. Their primary power is their dynamics. Keep them updated and visually show that things are being acted upon. Add new opportunities when new studies uncover new things. Keep discussing the items on the list with your stakeholders.

Some communication skills are not taught in any university program. The next section discusses a few of these "soft" communication skills, which can help you get stakeholder buy-in for UX research.

Soft communication skills
ALWAYS communicate what works well

Keeping a positive attitude is probably one of the most effective communication tools you have. It is easier to communicate bad news when opening with the good news first. After all, it is almost impossible to run a study and uncover only bad things. Another good reason to communicate what works well with a product or a design first is that you don't want people to mistakenly "fix" things that work well. Stakeholders sometimes are so affected by bad news studies that they want to change almost everything. It is important to communicate what works well to preserve these areas and to make sure they serve as examples or best practices for future efforts.

Another thing to remember when communicating what works well is that if you are listing things of minor importance, you are in fact communicating a message that the product is all bad. It will be perceived as if you have made an effort to find good aspects of a product but failed. You must find big, meaningful things that are working well. Plan to identify these things in advance. If, during a study session, you realize that nothing is working well for a participant, ask them to tell you what made them happy, what they value in the design they have just evaluated, or what things they want you to keep as is and not change at all.

Opportunities for improvement count for the vast majority of a study report. I try to have from 10 to 30 percent of the report specify positive findings. In some cases, especially if you are running studies as a part of an iterative design effort, you will find more positive things than usability issues.

The bottom line is that you should carefully craft a meaningful positive part to each and every one of your reports, presentations, and any other way you choose to communicate research results. Although it is key to report good news, it is the bad news that we UX practitioners need to communicate with great care, empathy, and attention to detail.

Become immersed in your team

The following techniques will help you become immersed in your team and become one of them, even though your discipline is very different than everybody else's:

1. **Attend social events and team celebrations.** Your team won a prize? Everybody goes to drink? A team New Year's toast was scheduled? Try to attend all of these. It is important that you have face time with everybody in the team – not just when you communicate research results, but also at social and team occasions.

2. **Be there during hard times.** Showing your face also applies in tough times. Be there when a crisis is happening. Offer help when your team suffers through hard times. Be one of the people who try to solve problems and move forward while keeping a positive, optimistic attitude.

3. **Walk the walk** (figure 5.23). This one works like magic. In short, when you arrive at the office in the morning, grab your coffee and walk a route that gives you a chance to say good morning and have some small talk with team members. Don't go directly to your cubicle and hide behind your monitor. Again, face time!

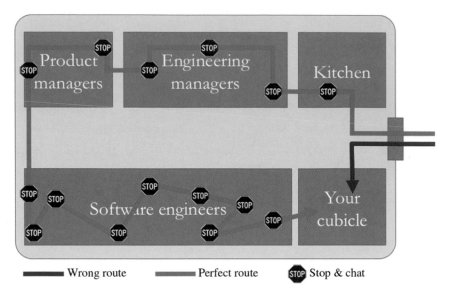

Figure 5.23: Walk the walk.

Communicate bad news

Bad news delivers the message that something is not working for someone as intended. For example, "Users don't understand what the company does after they spend two minutes in the home page." Or, "Users become extremely frustrated and think things are inefficient when they try to sign up for auto payment services." Or, "Users don't add a photo to their profile, either because they can't find where they can do it or because they don't see any value in it."

One of the biggest challenges for a UX researcher is telling someone that the product of their hard work is not good enough or that they were just wrong, then expecting them to fix it or change their opinion based on what "experts" say. The way you communicate bad news to people who have worked hard on something is critical. As much as it depends on you, it also depends on the receiving end of communication. It matters a lot if the software developers think they did an excellent job in designing a product or if they acknowledge they are not highly skilled designers. As you become immersed in your team, it is extremely important that you identify each person's skills and personality type. It'll help you in the way you communicate with them – especially when you communicate bad news. Immersion is key. If you are immersed within a team, they will not consider you to be an external consultant once they get to know you and trust you.

 Watch a fascinating interview with Chris St. Hilaire, author of *27 Powers of Persuasion*, from Los Angeles. Chris suggests that UX researchers recognize their stakeholders' pre-dispositions before they try to persuade them of anything. It's always easier to persuade someone about something they already believe. Use QR code 134 to access the video, a quick summary of the interview, and Chris's biography.

When you communicate bad news, follow these guidelines:

1. **Talk about what was found**, not about who designed something. When you focus on discussing findings, you are carrying a message that users are what's at stake here, not the good or bad job someone in the team did. For example, discuss why users could not find something and what can be done to improve it instead of trash-talking the information architecture. To be more specific, talk about things in the information architecture that caused users to get lost, such as labels that confused them, items that were placed under categories users did not expect to look for, and so on.

2. **Explain why these issues are bad news and use the language of business.** Designs and products usually have business goals, even if the organization is nonprofit. People who use these products have goals, too. Hopefully for the organization that develops products, the business and user goals complete or somehow match each other. When you explain why something is a problem, do it with this attitude of business and user goals and why users cannot achieve them with the current design unless it is changed.

3. **Never, ever make it personal.** Although it may seem so from time to time, it's not about anyone's personal opinion. Never say "I think." Instead, turn to higher authorities. Explain the principles you are using, provide supporting data from past studies you conducted, quote external resources if needed. Never point fingers. Never make it about someone doing a lousy job. In almost 100 percent of the cases, people want to do a better job with their designs. Most of them do their best. Making bad news personal is probably one of the biggest mistakes you can make.

TAKING ADVANTAGE OF THE THEORY OF PSYCHOLOGY AND HUMAN FACTORS

Beverly Freeman, Senior User Experience Researcher, eBay, United States

I always point out basic principles from psychology or human factors when predicting or reporting on research results. As one of my professors always says, non-human factors people who do usability testing have only data from that lab study to draw from, but trained human factors professionals know how to interpret empirical data based on a rich foundation. The more we can couch what we have to say in terms of our training, the more we can establish the fact that we are experts, not just lab monkeys.

Never use an escalation mandate

If you are given a mandate by upper management to escalate when people in your team do not follow research results, use it with care. Actually, never use it at all. The day you use that mandate will be the last day people buy in to research. Nothing good can happen after you escalate to executives. I once worked as a researcher in a company with about 600 software engineers. I was the sole UX practitioner there. Shortly after I joined the company, I had a one-on-one meeting with the vice president of R&D. That person told me that I had a full mandate to come and talk with her when my team gave me trouble with research – specifically, if they didn't listen to my recommendations. At first I thought to myself, "Wow, this company really cares about the user experience." But then I felt really bad. I imagined a situation during which I was not able to persuade stakeholders to follow one of my recommendations and what would happen if I escalated. I knew that 600 engineers would find out about such a meeting shortly after it happened. Needless to say, I never even thought of using this mandate.

Proxy designers

When researchers have strong, opinionated teams of engineers and product managers, carefully consider trying a technique called "proxy designers." What it basically means is that research findings and recommendations are pitched not to development teams, but to designers. Instead of negotiating with software engineers and product managers, the UX researcher works closely and solely with a designer. The designer designs the product based on their negotiations with the researcher and delivers it to the development team. Teams are not aware that research was done, but the design encompasses research results.

This technique has many disadvantages and very few advantages. It is great because it eliminates furious arguments and clashes between opinionated individuals and researchers. It is not so good because it indicates a very unhealthy environment, especially if a researcher needs to implement this technique on an ongoing basis. There's nothing wrong with it if you use it here and there, but if you do that all the time, it means that research is not respected in your organization and that something else needs to be done to defuse the situation.

 Watch my interview with Paul Adams, a product manager at Facebook and former UX researcher. Paul tells about a time when he had weaker relationships with his team and used designers as proxies for his research. Use QR code 112 to access the video, a quick summary of the interview, and Paul's biography.

REFERENCES

Csikszentmihalyi, M., 2004. Mihaly Csikszentmihalyi on flow. *TED.com.* <http://www.ted.com/talks/lang/eng/mihaly_csikszentmihalyi_on_flow.html> (accessed 02.16.11).

Molich, R., 2010. Usability test of <www.towerrecords.com>. <http://www.dialogdesign.dk/tekster/Tower_Test_Report.pdf> (accessed 09.08.11).

Nielsen, J., 1994. Usability Engineering. Morgan Kaufmann, San Francisco.

Quesenbery, W., Brooks, K., 2010. Storytelling for User Experience. Rosenfeld Media, New York.

Reynolds, G., 2008. Presentation Zen. New Riders, Berkeley, CA.

Tufte, E., 2005. The cognitive style of PowerPoint: Pitching out corrupts within. <http://www.edwardtufte.com/tufte/books_pp> (accessed 01.03.11).

Tullis, T., Albert, B., 2008. Measuring the User Experience: Collecting, Analyzing, and Presenting Usability Metrics. Morgan Kaufman, Burlington, MA.

Wilson, C., Pernice Coyne, K., 2001. The whiteboard: Tracking usability issues: To bug or not to bug? Interactions 8 (3), 15–19.

Wilson, C., 1999. Reader's questions: Severity scale for classifying usability problems. <http://www.stcsig.org/usability/newsletter/9904-severity-scale.html> (accessed 09.06.11).

TAKEAWAYS

This chapter is long. Therefore, it is important to highlight key takeaways of tactics and strategies for communicating via reports, presentations, videos, posters, and visualizations and by demonstrating effective soft communication skills:

1. Look deep down and think: do your stakeholders really need reports? Reports help crystallize key findings; they help create a presentation; they are a resource for the future; they make good references and include lots of data; and they are expected. On the other hand, they are slow to produce, static, passive, and silent; they have short shelf lives; they are not really sexy; and, like it or not, nobody reads them.

2. Avoid the report-which-is-actually-a-presentation. Decide on a form factor that is most suitable and go with it.

3. Share parts of the report with selected stakeholders and get their feedback before the final report is ready.

4. Always open a report with an executive summary that includes an opening paragraph with details of what was done, when, where, by whom, and why; a list of three positive findings; and a list of three opportunities for improvement.

5. Organize the report by research questions.

6. Don't report more than ten high-severity opportunities for improvement. Don't report medium- and low-severity opportunities if you don't have to.

7. Write short reports of up to five pages and long reports of up to ten pages.

8. Allow your key stakeholders to respond to the findings and recommendations in the report before you make it available to the entire team. Then share it with the team. Be transparent.

9. When you present research results, use stories, videos, pictures, and artifacts.

10. Try presenting with pictures.

11. When it comes to presentations, practice, practice, practice.

12. Present to your biggest critic privately, letting him or her poke holes in your presentation.

13. Run an expo.

14. Integrate qualitative and quantitative findings and tell compelling stories.

15. Communicate good news first and slowly, and bad news last and quickly.

16. Become immersed in your team. Walk the morning walk.

CHAPTER 6

You can't manage what you don't measure

SIGNS THAT INDICATE RESEARCH IS BEING USED WELL
AND HOW YOU CAN SYSTEMATICALLY TRACK SUCCESS (OR
FAILURE)

Livia Labate

President of the company explaining what an
ethnograhic study is during All Hands Meeting.
My work here is done.

Introduction

Think about the reasons that people and organizations decide to conduct UX research. Why are they doing this? Why all the effort? The number one reason they do it is because they want to learn about what their customers want and to make necessary changes to achieve that. When stakeholders act on research, you can clearly point to the positive effect that UX research is having on the organization, its products, and its customers. All you need to do is pay attention and be aware.

You can tell whether or not stakeholders act upon UX research results if you notice, track, and monitor their actions. Pay attention to what your stakeholders are saying about and doing with research results. By monitoring factors such as consumption of research, allocation of more funding, signs of stakeholder trust in UX research, changes the organization is making, and recognition researchers (or you) are getting, you can better understand what is working well and what needs to be improved with your practice. By tracking the status and the decisions made by stakeholders based on research, you can inform yourself about areas that require your attention.

This chapter identifies nine signs of stakeholder buy-in for research and offers practical techniques for monitoring agreement.

Signs that research is being used well

One of the hardest things to measure is how much your stakeholders buy in to UX research. There is no clear, quantifiable answer to this question. In one of my recent conference appearances, I was asked this question about stakeholder buy-in: "What does winning look like when it goes wonderfully right? Horribly wrong?" I thought about it a little bit and came up with nine signs that your stakeholders have bought into UX research. Here is what winning looks like when it goes wonderfully right:

1. Research is consumed.

2. Budget is allocated for more research.

3. Findings are long and lasting.

4. Trust is established.

5. Skeptical stakeholders become believers.

6. Business is changed.

7. Staffing is changed.

8. Repeated requests are made for UX research training.

9. Researchers are recognized.

If you see evidence of at least two or three of these signs, you can say that your stakeholders have bought into UX research. On the other hand, if you identify one or none of those signs, things are not going so well. Let's discuss the signs.

Research is consumed

A great indication of research uptake is that research recommendations – especially the most important ones – are followed. The most basic example of research consumption is when a problem that was uncovered during a research activity was solved or fixed as a result of the study. If stakeholders choose to fix only the problems that are easy to solve, that's one thing. A better indication of consumption is when they deal with fixing big problems identified during research. When significant changes are made to product design following research, that's a great sign for research consumption.

 Watch my interview with Giles Colborne, author of *Simple and Usable*, Managing Director of cxpartners, and former president of the UK UPA (Usability Professionals' Association). Giles argues that you are successful if you shift people's point of view of customers and how they use products. Use QR code 126 to access the video, a quick summary of the interview, and Giles's biography.

Another sign – less meaningful, yet favorable – of research consumption is when the company's representatives are using the company's investment in user research as a part of the sales pitch. When heat maps from your recent eye-tracking study are shown to potential customers, it's a sign that the company wants to show that it is serious about design. It does not necessarily mean that this is the case, but it is a positive indication that stakeholders perceive research as a unique selling proposition. If people are using research to tell customers how good a job the company is doing when in reality the research recommendations aren't followed, that stinks. In such cases, UX is seen as a way to dupe customers. If this happens a lot to you, I suggest that you refer to Chapter 1's discussion about difficult people, teams, and organizations.

This story from Italy starts by describing a standard usability study and has a surprising ending about how UX research can become a unique selling proposition.

BETTER BUYING EXPERIENCE FOR BLACKBERRY PHONES

Michele Visciola, General Manager, Experientia, Italy

When Research in Motion (RIM) asked Experientia to improve the out-of-the-box experience for Blackberry phones, we knew it was vital that our testing processes were as realistic as possible. We needed to explore the entire experience of purchasing a smartphone in a retail environment; we decided that the best way to do so was to simulate a full purchasing process, then put participants in our usability lab to see what really happened after the purchase.

"Out of the box" involved two distinct phases: (1) onsite observations carried out in mobile phone shops and showrooms, and (2) usability testing in the Experientia lab.

The findings of the research gave RIM information on participants' emotional reactions and satisfaction with the purchase and unboxing experience. As six models of phones were benchmarked, RIM could clearly see how the Blackberry products compared with competitors.

We presented recommendations for both project phases, including suggestions on point of sale information, packaging, improving the purchase experience, and making the configuration and interface of the phone more user-friendly and navigable. RIM thought our findings were so important that it turned them into a white paper, which it distributed to its sales points worldwide.

Many research reports have been admired for their correctness but then ultimately ignored when making product decisions. A white paper might not always be a good sign. It's up to you and your stakeholders to ensure that such a report is backed up by action.

Budget is allocated for more research

Success means that stakeholders or clients who have experienced UX research and enjoyed its benefits allocate more funding. It is a great sign when it comes from people, teams, and organizations you have already worked with before – and even more so when it is coming from people new to research. The latter means that rumors about UX research are spreading, which is definitely a good sign.

 Watch my interview with Kim Goodwin, author of *Designing for the Digital Age* and independent consultant. Kim says that when stakeholders budget for more research, that's the best sign for you that they have bought into it. Use QR code 124 to access the video, a quick summary of the interview, and Kim's biography.

Findings are long and lasting

The nature of generative research is that study results have long shelf life. These are usually the studies that have goals such as identifying user needs or uncovering who the users are. Chances are good that findings from these studies will remain valid and true for long periods of time. When I reflect on generative studies that I have conducted in the past, I see that they have had shelf lives of a few years. The reason, I believe, is that findings that emerge from that type of research relate more to human behavior and human nature, which tend not to change too often. An example would be the study mentioned in Chapter 5 in the discussion about running a research expo. That study had a goal of identifying the users of a product the company wanted to develop and their needs. Findings from this study lasted and were used for more than two years after it was completed because the basic needs of users in that realm did not change and will probably not change dramatically in the future.

Methodology is not always the factor that determines the length of shelf life of a research project. Sometimes it is the research goal that sets it. For instance, different stakeholders might use results of a study that compares the efficiency of two competing designs or products for long periods of time.

When study results are used and consumed by stakeholders for a long time after it has been completed, that is a good indicator for success. When this use does not happen, it might mean that something went wrong with planning, collaboration, and communication. It might also mean that stakeholders internalized study findings so well that they now think it is something they have always known.

Trust is established

One of the most frustrating things that can happen to a UX researcher is realizing that stakeholders do not trust his or her work. It is probably very rare that stakeholders will say they don't trust your work to your face. On the other hand, one of the most encouraging things a UX researcher can experience is when trust is established with stakeholders. In companies where people frequently move on to other positions, you are faced with having to establish trust all over again with new stakeholders. There are two clear signs for established trust. It is important for me to emphasize that the absence of these signs does not mean your stakeholders do not trust you. It might, but there is no single sign for it. The two signs are:

> **Researchers are invited to important discussions.** When people want to hear what you have to say, it is usually a good sign that trust is being established. When you get a seat at the table where important decisions are being made, that's a great sign. I realize that UX researchers are rarely invited to *the* table. But – and this is a big "but" – more and more companies now realize that they need to make the table bigger so that it includes UX people.

Teams want to work with researchers. When UX research is having an impact, people talk with each other about it. It is not uncommon to see "new business" arriving at the doorstep of UX researchers who make an impact. It could start with an email, an IM conversation, or a hallway chitchat. Or it could show up as a formal request for additional UX research staff members or an allocation that is temporary or permanent. When more teams want to work with UX researchers, that's usually a good sign of buy-in for research. Whether to positively respond to these requests is another issue. If UX management topics interest you, I recommend Arnie Lund's *User Experience Management: Essential Skills for Leading UX Teams* (2011).

Skeptical stakeholders become believers

One of the best moments as a UX or usability practitioner is when a stakeholder gets it. There's that spark in their eyes that tells you they believe. It doesn't happen often, but when it does – especially if those stakeholders are senior decision makers or executives – that spark in their eyes can move mountains for you and for the UX practice in the organization you work for.

The following is a story about such a moment.

What Happened When I Invited Executives to Use the Product?

I worked for a mature startup at the beginning of my career. I can divide my time there into two big parts; before and after a certain usability study. Prior to that study, I was mainly struggling with my stakeholders, especially with executives and the two founders of the startup. They were very opinionated about design issues, big and small. They preferred to rely on their own intuition rather than on research findings and recommendations. The primary product that the company developed has had many design flaws that were consistently overlooked by management. It was very clear to me that they needed to experience what users were going through and I had found the way to do just that.

In the spirit of "show, don't tell," I decided to stop talking about UX research and advocating for our users. Instead, I designed a usability study around the primary tasks that our users need to complete with the product. The twist was that I did not recruit users to participate in this study. Instead, I invited members of the company's executive team to act as users and participate. During the study, executives were not able to use our product and were not successful at completing basic tasks. I did not have a goal to learn anything about the design of the product. I learned everything I needed to learn about the design from past research with product users. My goal was to prove a point. This exercise resulted in several quick decisions. First, the product roadmap was changed and an overall redesign plan was put in place. That result definitely matched my expectations. The second decision surprised me. The executive management team asked me to take the position of product manager for the redesign while conducting any UX research I deemed appropriate. I hesitated for a moment, and then decided to go for it.

Business is changed

The following signs might tell you that the business is changing due to UX research:

Business decisions are based on research findings. Strategic partners are sought, acquisitions are made, mergers happen, and new target audiences are defined. When these things happen after someone made a decision based on user research, that's a huge indicator of success.

Product roadmaps are reshaped. When product decisions – such as developing new, significant features or investing in more research or stopping a launch of a faulty product – are made based on UX research, you can say that research has made its mark.

New products are born based on research recommendations. Sometimes research points out new opportunities for developing products. One study will not cause people to decide to develop a new product, but a research program combined with market research and collaboration with other people and departments in the organization can make this happen.

Watch my interview with Aza Raskin, cofounder of Massive Health, who was until recently Creative Lead for Firefox. Previously, he was a founding member of Mozilla Labs. Aza says that when decisions are being made, research is being listened to. That's the clearest sign. Use QR code 113 to access the video, a quick summary of the interview, and Aza's biography.

Staffing is changed

Two positive signs of UX research effects on stakeholders relate to staffing:

Engineers are allocated to act upon research recommendations. When managers decide to dedicate teams' or individuals' time to act upon research, that's a great success. People can be allocated to fix bugs, solve design issues, implement improved designs, develop new features, and even work on new products – all stemming from research. I refer specifically to engineers because they are the ones who can actually make changes to products. When more designers, product managers, and researchers are allocated to solve problems that emerge from UX research, that is really, noncynically awesome, but engineers are the frontline troops that make things happen.

Job descriptions emphasize UX skills. I'm a great believer in specialization. I think people should know a lot about one thing and a little about many things. But when I see the following requirement appearing on the top of a job description for a product manager in my team, it warms my heart: "Fight for the user. As a product manager, you drive the team to achieve excellence in usability, look and feel, and fit and finish." This means that your team's leadership appreciates what UX has to offer and is actively seeking to hire people with a mind open to UX in general, and, more specifically, to research.

Repeated requests are made for UX research training

An important sign is when stakeholders make repeated requests to go through some kind of training that would help them become better at quick research. My experience with these training requests shows that stakeholders usually want to learn the following:

- How to interpret research results
- How to do a better job interviewing users

- How to better phrase survey questions
- How to run quick usability tests

Researchers are recognized

A good word or an award given to a UX researcher individually or as a part of a team is a sign of a mature organization that understands the importance and contribution of research to its operations and product development. Know these "hey-we-launched-X-thank-you-everyone" emails that name all the people who were involved in a certain effort? When UX researchers are recognized in such emails, there's a good reason to celebrate. It means people see you, and UX research, as an integral part of the team.

Now that you know some signs that your research is being used well, how do you improve the chances of your research being perceived as having an impact? When you plan research activities based on listening to your stakeholders (see Chapters 2 and 3), when you collaborate with them throughout the process (see Chapter 4), and when you communicate results well (Chapter 5), you are on the right track.

Next, I'll introduce some techniques that will help you track the impact you are making with research.

How to track the impact of research
Have a buy-in tracking strategy

Don't just sit back, do your job, and assume that people will get engaged because you are bringing such great value with your research. Yes, more and more stake-holders worldwide get it and understand how important it is to conduct UX research and act upon its results. But many don't. And chances are good that you are or will be working with stakeholders who don't get it. You should make it a habit to think, plan, execute, measure, and track your stakeholder buy-in level for research. Whether it is taking 25 percent or 50 percent of your time or if your manager does (or should do) it, you need to put time aside for making your research count. Conducting extraordinary, high-quality research is very important, but if it doesn't count – if people don't act upon it – it isn't worth much.

This section introduces some techniques for tracking the effectiveness of UX research in your organization or with your clients. I don't prescribe all of these techniques for all practitioners in every situation. Feel free to mix and match, develop your own techniques, and use any or all of these. The most important thing to do with these techniques is share their outcomes with your stakeholders. I'm not suggesting that you track your stakeholder buy-in so you can make a case when people ask you how effective your research is. Instead, I strongly encourage you to use these issues with your team or clients. For example, don't wait for people to ask you what the effect of the study was on the design. Instead, show before and after screenshots to your stakeholders. When you do that on a regular basis, no one will doubt the value of UX research.

Before and after screenshots

Before and after images have a tremendous effect. Ask any advertising manager who has used before and after ads. Ask anyone who's lost a lot of weight. These images are also extremely valuable as a tracking tool. If you haven't tracked UX research impact with before and after screenshots, you'll be amazed at their value. There are two things to be aware of when you use this technique. The first is not to use an "after" image that is too far from the "before" image. The next three examples demonstrate what I mean.

Usabilitynet.org is a website that was launched in 2003 to organize information and resources for usability practitioners. Figure 6.1 is a screenshot of the site's home page. This is the "before" screenshot. Figure 6.2 is a sample of a redesigned version of the home page, which is based on research findings. The number-one thing to be aware of when using before and after screenshots is that it is not always clear how the changes in the redesign are mapped to research findings. It is up to you to make sure that it is very clear. You can associate the changes with the research by adding callouts or by listing the research findings that affected each design change.

The Usability Body of Knowledge (BoK; Usabilitybok.org) is a project led by UPA (Usability Professionals' Association) to serve as a living reference that represents the collective knowledge of the usability profession (Usabilitybok.org 2011). The project was launched in 2005. The BoK can be considered a redesign or a better version of

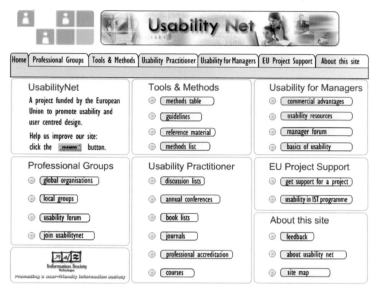

Study participants had trouble with the original design for these topics. They got confused by the images that looked like radio buttons and the button design of the links. Therefore, all links changed to the standard blue underlined text.

Study participants did not quickly understand the purpose of the site. The tagline was moved from bottom to the top of the page to a more visible and standard location.

Participants felt that the original design was overwhelming and overloaded. This design includes more white space and less clutter. It also follows strict alignment to grid lines.

the Usabilitynet.org website. For the sake of the example, let's assume this is the case. When you look at the site's home page (see figure 6.3), you can pretty quickly see that it is very different from Usabilitynet.org, which brings me to the second thing you need to be aware of when you use before and after screenshots. When the delta between the before and after designs is too great, it is hard to understand that this is actually an "after" image. It would probably seem to stakeholders like a completely new design, which in many cases it actually is. Again, there will be a challenge with mapping research findings to the actual design. A better way would be to use only the "after" screenshot and use callouts to track what came from research.

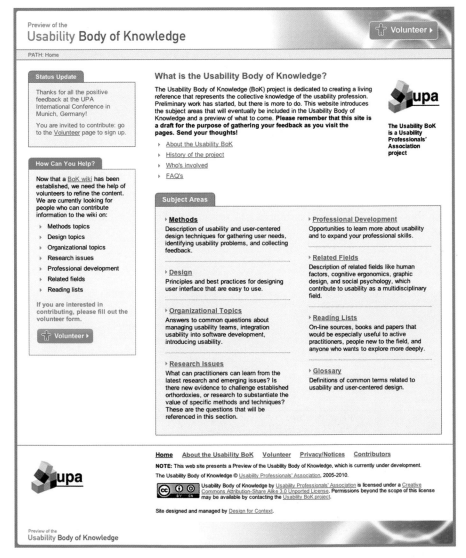

Figure 6.3:
Usabilitybok.org:
a possible "after"
screenshot.

Screenshots with callouts

Probably one of the most effective visual manners for tracking stakeholder buy-in for research is a screenshot with callouts. If your product does not have a screen, you can also use this technique if you take a picture of it (see Figure 6.4). The screenshot can be taken from the version that was evaluated during the study or after study results are implemented. Callouts might point out findings and recommendations that were fixed or not fixed. Figure 6.5 shows an example of both.

Screenshots with callouts are a great tool for tracking research buy-in. A quick glance allows you and your stakeholders to understand what was done, what wasn't, and what should be done next. You can print all these screenshots in color and hang them on the walls around you and your team. This way, you can put a big green checkmark on each callout to indicate that it has been taken care of. That's a great visual way to follow up on research results.

Screenshots with callouts are a great tool for tracking not only what happened in a study, but also why it happened, as described in the following story. Understanding why something happened usually helps stakeholders make the correct design changes and prevents them from making design mistakes in the future.

Figure 6.4:
Using callouts with a picture of a physical product.

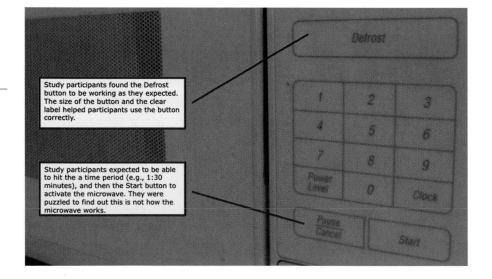

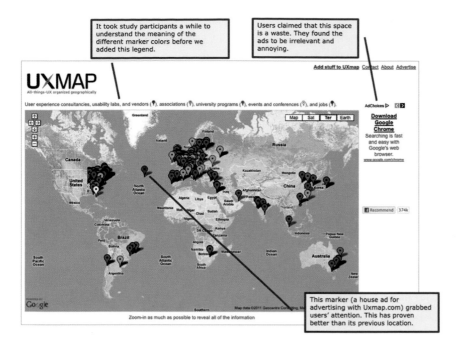

Figure 6.5: Using callouts with a digital product.

WHY?

Agnieszka (Aga) Bojko, Associate Director, User Centric, Inc., United States

I often see usability reports in which findings are listed only in terms of what happened during test sessions: "Five out of twelve participants did this . . . Two could not do that . . . Most said this . . . Some mentioned that . . . ." It makes me wonder how much the stakeholders actually get out of reports like that.

I recently talked to an executive at a hardware ecommerce website. "The reason I dropped $50K on this study was not just to learn about what people do, but more importantly, why," he said with disappointment as he handed me the report he received from the firm that conducted the study.

One of the main findings stated, "Most participants didn't realize that they were supposed to create their password on the order confirmation page." That was it. Several questions immediately came to mind. Was it because of the location of the password creation prompt on the page? Was it because of its location in the process? Was it because of the way it was presented? Or was it due to unclear instructions? However, the document didn't even entertain any of these possibilities.

The problem of "why"-less reports is even further exacerbated by the fact that stakeholders sometimes explicitly ask for the *what* with little care for the *why*. Let's take eye-tracking studies as an example. If I had a dime for every time I heard, "We just want to know where people are looking" as a study objective, I could buy myself another eye tracker. However, many researchers do what they are told – they determine where participants' eyes are fixated and present the results as numbers in tables, graphs, or heat maps. Only after the findings reach the stakeholders do they realize that something is missing.

What does it matter that most participants looked for the Submit button on the right side of the screen when in fact it was located on the left? What does that mean? Was it because participants expected to see it on the right? Because there was something else on the right that looked like a Submit button? Or perhaps because they were distracted by something that was unrelated but was also located on the right?

Without articulating potential sources of the usability problems found, usability reports provide very little value, for two reasons. First, stakeholders will not know which design mistakes they should avoid in the future. Second, if the recommendations provided in the report are not feasible, without understanding what in the design caused the problem stakeholders won't be able to come up with alternative solutions. Therefore, if we want to provide value, it is our job as UX researchers to always present the *why* with the *what*.

Spreadsheets

Probably the most popular technique for tracking engagement of stakeholders with research is with a straightforward spreadsheet that lists the issues that were uncovered in research while indicating what is going to be done about them, by whom, and when. This spreadsheet usually serves as a team collaboration tool for tracking the status of research results. This spreadsheet is also pretty useful when people ask to see a list of the most updated research findings and their status. Keep in mind that this spreadsheet is a live, dynamic document that is constantly updated. The trick is to get the information. It's a very easy task if you are well immersed within your team, more difficult if you are not.

Table 6.1 Sample research follow-up spreadsheet				
Finding	**Solution**	**Target fix date**	**Owner**	**Status**
Users tend to use search queries with an average of 38 characters. Our box is 17 characters long, which makes users futz with the query for too long and get annoyed with us.	Increase the width of the search box to 40 visible characters.	Q1	Jane Smith	In progress
Users did not know what the lead story was.	Increase the lead story image and headline size while decreasing the equivalent sizes of the second story.	Q1	N/A	No owner
It took a while before study participants were able to tell when the site was last updated.	Brainstorm a better location for the last update time. A good example: nytimes.com	Q2	Ginny Bell	Launched

Table 6.1 is an example of what such a spreadsheet might look like.

You can be creative with using background colors to indicate the status and severity of listed issues, but don't overdo it. The spreadsheet needs to be straightforward and crystal clear. You can of course add more columns and details such as ease of implementation, whether the team agrees to the solution, and other details. The minimum is probably four columns: solution, target fix date, owner, and status. I have some stakeholders who are not interested in learning what the findings were. They trust me to reach the right solutions and don't bother reading reports. They only care about what they should do to make things better. Needless to say, I highly appreciate this approach. For this state of mind, a spreadsheet is probably the most effective report and tracking tool. One other suggestion is to not develop this spreadsheet as a separate file. Instead, include it as a table at the end of the research report (if you prepared one). This way, it is easy for everyone involved to find and access it.

Quotes and videos

Stakeholder quotes and videos are a powerful tool for tracking stakeholder buy-in for research. Here are some ideas for collecting stakeholder quotes and videos:

- Company-wide or division-wide (if you work in a large organization) meetings at which chief officers talk about UX and UX research.
- Key stakeholder reactions, especially first reactions, to research results. Usually the best place to get these is during your presentations.

- "Invited" responses to research results. Shortly after you share research results, directly approach key stakeholders face to face, by phone, or in email and ask them how useful they think the results are.

- Product marketing materials. These often tend to highlight UX research as a unique selling point.

- Stakeholder speeches in professional conferences and at big client events. If you are doing a great job of engaging your stakeholders, they will be proud of UX research and will present highlights of your work externally.

- Email updates and messages sent to teams or to the entire company by key stakeholders and executives.

When the quotes include positive mentions of UX research, that is obviously a very good sign that your stakeholders are engaged with research. The fact of the matter is that even if they say the UX of the company's products is not very well done, it is positive, in a way. It presents opportunities for pitching and conducting effective research with the goal of changing the current situation. It's what you make of it that matters.

 Watch my interview with Johanna Kollmann, Senior UX Consultant at EMC Consulting. Johanna says you know that stakeholders have bought into research when they tell other people stories that came from research. Use QR code 131 to access the video, a quick summary of the interview, and Johanna's biography.

The primary thing you can do with all of these videos and quotes is collect them in one place. This collection will help you get a better picture of the level of buy-in your stakeholders have with UX research. Nothing about it is quantitative. I can't really say that if the CEO says UX research is great three times per quarter rather than five, it means you are not doing a good job. It is a qualitative measure that must be combined with many other buy-in signals.

Research analytics

If you use a website, internal or external, that allows stakeholders to view research results or artifacts, I highly recommend that you use a web analytics service to monitor its traffic. Of course, as with every analytics service, you will uncover only what is happening in terms of traffic, not why. To know why traffic is changing for better or worse, you'll need to add more qualitative approaches to monitoring engagement, such as the ones described so far.

The analytics service will not only tell you the traffic volume but will also help you understand where it is coming from. If your research results audience is international, this information can tell you whether the right people or offices of your company are interested in research. In addition, the time that people spend on your results site pages might be useful in understanding what is going on. Another important metric that an analytics service can provide is the bounce rate, or the percentage of site visitors who bounce away to a different website rather than continue exploring the site they are currently visiting. If you have an 85 percent bounce rate from your research report home page, it means that visitors were interested in the results, and hence accessed the site, but were discouraged from exploring them after they saw the content of the home page. There's definitely more for you to explore about what you can do better if you identify such behavior.

REFERENCES

Lund, A., 2011. User Experience Management: Essential Skills for Leading UX Teams. Morgan Kaufmann, Waltham, MA.

Usabilitybok.org, 2011. Usability body of knowledge. <http://www.usabilitybok.org> (accessed 06.22.11).

TAKEAWAYS

In this chapter, I discussed ways to measure and track stakeholder buy-in for user experience research:

1. If you conduct UX research to drive change, you must develop ways to determine whether change is happening.
2. Pay attention to how your stakeholders consume research results.
3. A very clear sign of success is the allocation of funds to and sponsorship of UX research.
4. If stakeholders care about your opinions, it's a good sign of trust.
5. When people are assigned to make changes that stem from research, that's a great positive signal.
6. Use before and after screenshots of product designs to track research effectiveness.
7. Use a simple spreadsheet to track the implementation of research results.
8. Collect responses to research, both qualitative (stakeholder quotes and videos) and quantitative (web analytics for research reports).

EPILOGUE

A ship is safe in harbor, but that's not what ships
are for. —William Shedd

Last piece of advice: if you want buy-in, do a great job

It's important to get stakeholders to buy into UX research. It is even more important to do high-quality research work. You cannot get buy-in from stakeholders for crappy research. Invest more in becoming a knowledgeable researcher and in performing high-quality, relevant research. This work will serve you well and will become a solid foundation for stakeholders to be more involved, engaged, and appreciative of the value of your work.

The final story in this book demonstrates how important it is for UX research work to meet high standards.

QUALITY AND USABILITY

Rolf Molich, Owner and Manager, DialogDesign, Denmark

To get stakeholder buy-in, usability professionals need to deliver useful and usable results. We must practice what we preach by paying attention to the quality, usefulness, and usability of our own products. Some of our procedures, such as usability testing, are no longer "anything-goes" works of art. Rather, they have become industrial processes that can and should be measured for efficiency, quality, and adherence to commonly accepted standards.

Clients have asked me to assess the quality of usability tests carried out for them by renowned usability agencies in eight countries all over the world. All quality assessments have been remote – I have not attended the actual test sessions. Assessments are based on usability test videos and test reports.

Clients want uniform and state-of-the-art usability tests across countries, including countries whose language they do not understand. They also want to be sure that they got what they paid for so that they can safely make important decisions based on the usability test results. Almost all the usability professionals involved in these tests had impressive portfolios and credentials from renowned universities.

The findings were interesting. Only one agency out of eight passed without serious issues. The rest all got one or more serious or critical markdowns on their adherence to generally accepted procedures for usability testing. No one has challenged the procedure or the findings or the assessor, so it seems that we have a generally accepted common body of knowledge.

Usability problems mainly showed up in the usability test reports:

- Unusable executive summaries – missing, too long, or vague
- Too long – the quality of a test report is not proportional to its length
- No positive findings

There were also usability problems in some highlight videos:

- Inadvertent help from moderator during test session, often because moderator talks too much
- Unrealistic test tasks or tasks with hidden clues
- Fewer participants than agreed with client – "If a test participant doesn't show up, that's the client's problem"

Attention to quality pays off. As the software guru Gerry Weinberg puts it, "If you don't care about quality, you can meet any other requirement."

INDEX